T0199693

Environment Art in the Game Industry

Environment Art in the Game Industry

A Guide to Rich and Realistic Environments Using Substance Designer

Henry Kelly

CRC Press
Taylor & Francis Group
Boca Raton London New York

CRC Press is an imprint of the
Taylor & Francis Group, an **informa** business

First edition published 2022
by CRC Press
6000 Broken Sound Parkway NW, Suite 300, Boca Raton, FL 33487-2742

and by CRC Press
2 Park Square, Milton Park, Abingdon, Oxon, OX14 4RN

© 2022 Taylor & Francis Group, LLC

CRC Press is an imprint of Taylor & Francis Group, LLC

ISBN: 9780367706791 (hbk)
ISBN: 9780367706760 (pbk)
ISBN: 9781003147497 (ebk)

DOI: 10.1201/9781003147497

Typeset in Minion
by codeMantra

In Loving Memory

Gillian Richards
26–04–1954 to 01–07–2019

I want to dedicate this book to:

My late Mother-in-Law

Gillian Richards,

My Father-in-Law

Eddie Richards

Nothing has made me work harder and opened my eyes up to family and what it means to want to work towards something.

You never gave up on me and are always impressed and proud of my artistic achievements.

My wife, Louise Kelly, for sticking with me through this journey and supporting my dreams of becoming an artist within the game industry.

And to my children, Amarah, Alexander, and Rosaura.

And my stepchildren, Faith, Isabella, and Toby.

Daddy loves you.

Contents

Acknowledgements

A big thanks to the Marmoset team for allowing me to use and adapt their 'Basic Theory of Physically-Based Rendering' by Jeff Russel: https://marmoset.co/posts/basic-theory-of-physically-based-rendering/.

Chris Peyton at Rebellion Developments for allowing me to use Mark Witts's 'Portfolio Pieces of Multiple-Level Blockouts to Final Dressing'.

Mark Witts for allowing me to use his Portfolio Pieces of Multiple Level Block outs to Final Dressing. Mark Witts' portfolio can be found at https://www.artstation.com/markwitts.

Luke Ahearn for his guidance throughout the journey of writing my first book and being honest!

Author

Henry Kelly has worked within the 3D Industry, part-time, from the age of 18, creating 3D models, improving his techniques and learning new material. After leaving the military, he took up 3D art full-time and began a career as a freelance Environment Artist, where he worked for independent and AAA game studios such as Crytek, Rebellion, Offworld industries amongst other smaller studios. Through the years, he climbed the ranks from a freelancer to a lead artist, maintaining his focus on Environment Art. He has contributed to new and exciting methods that speed up workflow and produce higher-quality artwork for games. Henry is an instructor for Master's and Bachelor's degree programs, and is responsible for writing the curriculum for both. In his spare time, he occasionally serves as an instructor for Ryan Kingslien, a renowned art sculptor and a major contributor to the game industry.

CHAPTER 1

Introduction

1.1 MY PROFESSIONAL CLIMB

I set myself one goal in life, to work in the game industry; over the years, I have developed and learned new skills regarding game development and art. I started out 3D modelling when I was just 14 years old for a virtual chat room/game called There (www.there.com). I then moved my skills over to another virtual chat room after around a year called Second Life, www.secondlife.com (which is still very booming). Over the years, I developed my ability to create 3D models and textures, it also helped that I sold my assets in Several Games and Websites. After a few years, whilst I was in the British Army, I decided to keep honing my skills as a 3D artist utilizing any chance that I had. I started Developing and Producing assets to sell on websites such as www.turbosquid.com and www.cgtrader.com.

I started freelancing for Small Indie studios around the age of 18, freelancing for a small team creating a game called Dinosaur Battlegrounds, which was quite fun. I then started working side by side with a Lead Producer at a Microsoft studio; whilst this was not directly involved with Microsoft, we were developing new techniques for creating 3D foliage and assets with Photogrammetry. (This was before Photogrammetry was as big in the industry.) Because I worked heavily on Photogrammetry with Andrew, I eventually started building my portfolio, which gained my foot into the game industry where I started at my first AA Studio at Gymcraft where I worked on the VR Title, FreeDriverVR, which was a VR fitness game now used across gyms all over China and Japan.

I then moved into AAA studio work at Rebellion Developments (www.rebellion.com).

DOI: 10.1201/9781003147497-1

I worked on multiple titles and techniques whilst I was working at Rebellion; I also improved my foliage production abilities quite a lot here. My responsibilities were to assist the Strange Brigade team towards the end of production by creating assets for cut scenes (a parachute and a giant door).

Some of my foliage was used on this project too.

During my course of working on Strange Brigade, I also worked on the final DLC for Sniper Elite 4 where I created small assets for gameplay purposes and other assets too.

I started working on the pre-production team for Zombie Army 4 and had my own level to work on; during this time, I was also working closely with the rest of my art team to develop new techniques with both Photogrammetry and Substance Designer/Painter.

After finding out that my mother-in-law had only a few months left to live after being diagnosed with cancer, I had to leave the studio which was one of my biggest regrets. I was approached by a studio called Offworld Industries where they offered me a job as a Senior Environment Artist working on games such as Squad and Post Scriptum.

Before starting this position, I was told that the Lead Artist was fired and the Lead Producer stepped down, and so the position was no longer available, but I was offered a lead role instead. I moved to Canada, because I could not do this, but I worked for a year on Squad and helped produce and finalize maps for AAA release.

After working a year, I decided to take a hiatus from the game industry and started teaching at a university in London at BA and MA levels. Here, I really improved my skills and learned quite a lot whilst also teaching students how to improve their artistic abilities and pay attention to the smaller details that make artists within this industry harder to come by.

Now, upon finishing this book, I am currently the Lead Artist at REWIND, a VR & AR Studio with the vision of a better future for VR & AR.

1.2 WHAT IS AN ENVIRONMENT ARTIST?

As an Environment Artist in the game industry, we face challenges daily. The reasons why we face these challenges are that there is not one area that is specific to an Environment Artist, and we usually have a 'specific skill' or an 'area' that we are specialized in. In my case, I am a 'Principal Foliage Artist', which means that although I am a Lead Environment Artist, I also specialize in foliage. Any principal artists usually have the most amount of knowledge of their speciality within that specific area.

Environment Art is one of the best areas to work in the game industry (from a biased perspective) because of the simple fact that as an Environment Artist, there are multiple areas covered on a daily basis. For example, working on Zombie Army 4, I was in charge of set dressing a specific level. I was also in charge of creating all of the textures/materials and the majority of assets for that level, and so to break it down, Environment Artists should have a great understanding of material workflow, set dressing and storytelling and should have an artistic eye for detail.

Before we go deeper into the role of an Environment Artist, I would like to clarify a few 'words' used.

1.3 WHAT IS SET DRESSING?

Set dressing is what an Environment Artist's main duty within any studio; once a Level Designer has 'blocked out' a level, they will then pass it across to an Environment Artist who will take the blocking out and add details, adding furniture, foliage, props and other elements to the environment and finalizing it into a full-fledged, detailed world.

Here, I will be using Rebellions images of Strange Brigade:

In the image below, you can see a White-boxed level; this is a level that is just metrically blocked out by a Level Designer to test gameplay techniques and ensure smooth transitions throughout the entire level.

After a Level Designer has gone through this process, it is handed off to an Environment Artist who will be solely (for the most part) responsible for creating the final looking scene.

In the image below, you can see how the process will develop over time: the first point of call to an Environment Artist is to add all of the scenery elements, buildings, trees, grass, bushes, cliffs, rock faces, water, etc. Then the Level Designer will come back in and add more information and details into the scene (the green areas represent areas where the player can 'climb' or 'vault').

After a while of working on materials and textures, adding more details and changing areas to look good, you will eventually end up with something that looks like the image below. This is how the majority of the set dressing is completed.

Another very nice feature from the White box to finish is this series of images below.

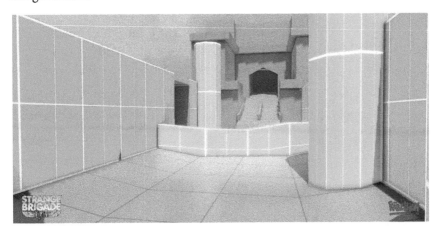

As you can see, throughout the process, different elements and also assets will change, but the majority of what you see in a level is created by an Environment Artist.

In other game studios such as Ubisoft, you will often find that the Environment Artist's role is broken down into a 'World Builder' role, whereas most of the work you will do is just simply set dressing scenes; this means that you do not have to create assets or materials. However, this can sometimes become dull and limit your artistic abilities.

CHAPTER 2

What Is PBR?

2.1 WHAT IS PBR (PHYSICALLY-BASED RENDERING)?

Just before we jump into breaking down what a material is, it is important to understand some of the words and context. So we need to understand more about PBR, 'physically-based rendering'.

PBR is an approach in computer graphics that more accurately lights and renders materials and objects as they would appear in the real world.

PBR was created to react in better lighting circumstances by eliminating shadows and highlights from textures, and instead, drawing/rendering these eliminations through computer software. Previously, the older technique involved had a 'diffuse' texture that would hold colour and shadow/highlight information for display/render.

See the image below:

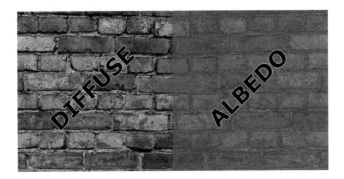

As you can see, the image on the left is a diffuse texture, an older method to rendering without PBR software; this technique holds the shadow and highlights information on the texture; you can see the shadows in the cavity and the brick highlights from the sun. However, on the right side you can see that all we have is colour information, which allows us to change the direction of the sun within the game engine, thus changing the shadow and highlight direction on the surface.

Let us take a look at the more technical side of this process, so that we can deeply understand what we are doing before we dive into Substance Designer.

The following is adapted from the 'Basic Theory of Physically-Based Rendering' by Jeff Russell (https://marmoset.co/posts/basic-theory-of-physically-based-rendering/) (used with permission).

2.2 DIFFUSION AND REFLECTION

Diffusion and reflection – also known as 'diffuse' and 'specular' light, respectively – are two terms describing the most basic separation of surface/light interactions. Most people will be familiar with these ideas on a practical level but may not know how they are physically distinct.

When light hits a surface boundary, some of it will reflect – that is, bounce off – from the surface and leave heading in a direction on the opposing side of the surface normal. This behaviour is very similar to a ball thrown against the ground or a wall – it will bounce off at the opposite angle. On a smooth surface, this will result in a mirror-like appearance. The word 'specular', often used to describe the effect, is derived from the Latin for 'mirror' (it seems that 'specularity' sounds less awkward than 'mirrorness').

Not all light reflects from a surface, however. Usually some will penetrate the interior of the illuminated object. There it will either be absorbed by the material (usually converting to heat) or scattered internally. Some of this scattered light may make its way back out of the surface, then becoming visible once more to eyeballs and cameras. This is known by many names: 'Diffuse Light', 'Diffusion' and 'Subsurface Scattering' – all describing the same effect.

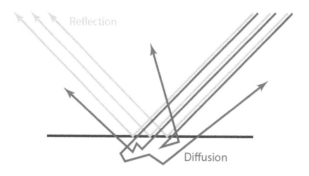

The absorption and scattering of diffuse light are often quite different for different wavelengths of light, which is what gives objects their colour (e.g. if an object absorbs most light but scatters blue, it will appear blue). The scattering is often so uniformly chaotic that it can be said to appear the same from all directions – quite different from the case of a mirror! A shader using this approximation just needs one input: 'albedo', a colour that describes the fractions of various colours of light that will scatter back out of a surface. 'Diffuse colour' is a phrase sometimes used synonymously.

2.3 TRANSLUCENCY AND TRANSPARENCY

In some cases, diffusion is more complicated – in materials that have wider scattering distances, for example, skin or wax. In these cases, a simple colour will usually not do, and the shading system must consider the shape and thickness of the object being lit. If they are thin enough, such objects often see light scattering out the backside and can then be called translucent. If the diffusion is even lower yet (for example, glass), then almost no scattering is evident at all and the entire image can pass through an object from one side to another intact. These behaviours are different enough from the typical 'close to the surface' diffusion that unique shaders are usually needed to simulate them.

2.4 ENERGY CONSERVATION

With these descriptions, we now have enough information to draw an important conclusion, which is that *reflection and diffusion are mutually exclusive*. This is because, for light to be diffused, light must first penetrate the surface (that is, fail to reflect). This is known in shading parlance as an example of 'energy conservation', which just means that the light leaving a surface is never any brighter than that which fell upon it originally.

This is easy to enforce in a shading system: one simply subtracts reflected light before allowing the diffuse shading to occur. This means highly reflective objects will show little to no diffuse light, simply because little to no light penetrates the surface, having been mostly reflected. The converse is also true: if an object has bright diffusion, it cannot be especially reflective.

Increasing Reflectivity
(Constant Albedo)

Energy conservation of this sort is an important aspect of physically-based shading. It allows the artist to work with reflectivity and albedo values for a material without accidentally violating the laws of physics (which tends to look bad). While enforcing these constraints in code is not strictly necessary to produce good-looking art, it does serve a useful role as a kind of 'nanny physicist' that will prevent the artwork from bending the rules too far or becoming inconsistent under different lighting conditions.

2.5 METALS

Electrically conductive materials, most notably metals, are deserving a special mention at this point for a few reasons.

Firstly, they tend to be much more reflective than insulators (non-conductors). Conductors will usually exhibit reflectivities as high as 60%–90%, whereas insulators are generally much lower, in the 0%–20% range. These high reflectivities prevent most light from reaching the interior and scattering, giving metals a very 'shiny' look.

Secondly, reflectivity on conductors will sometimes vary across the visible spectrum, which means that their reflections appear tinted. This colouring of reflection is rare even among conductors, but it does occur in some everyday materials (e.g. gold, copper and brass). Insulators as a rule do not exhibit this effect, and their reflections are uncoloured.

Finally, electrical conductors will usually absorb rather than scatter any light that penetrates the surface. This means that in theory, conductors will not show any evidence of diffuse light. In practice, however, there are often oxides or other residues on the surface of a metal that will scatter some small amounts of light.

It is this duality between metals and just about everything else that leads some rendering systems to adopt 'metalness' as a direct input. In such systems, artists specify the degree to which a material behaves as a metal, rather than specifying only the albedo and reflectivity explicitly. This is sometimes preferred as a simpler means of creating materials but is not necessarily a characteristic of physically-based rendering.

2.6 FRESNEL

Augustin-Jean Fresnel seems to be one of those old dead white guys we are unlikely to forget, mainly because his name is plastered on a range of phenomena that he was the first to accurately describe. It would be hard to discuss the reflection of light without mentioning his name.

In computer graphics, the word Fresnel refers to differing reflectivities that occur at different angles. Specifically, light that lands on a surface at a grazing angle will be much more likely to reflect than that hits a surface dead-on. This means that objects rendered with a proper Fresnel effect will appear to have brighter reflections near the edges. Most of us have been familiar with this for a while now, and its presence in computer graphics is not new. However, PBR shaders have made a few important corrections popular in the evaluation of Fresnel's equations.

The first is that for all materials, reflectivity becomes total for grazing angles – the 'edges' viewed on any smooth object should act as perfect (uncoloured) mirrors, no matter the material. Yes, really –*any substance can act as a perfect mirror* if it is smooth and viewed at the right angle! This can be counterintuitive, but the physics are clear.

The second observation about the Fresnel properties is that the curve or gradient between the angles does not vary much from material to material. Metals are the most divergent, but they too can be accounted for analytically.

What this means for us is that assuming realism is desired, artist control over the Fresnel behaviour should generally be *reduced*, rather than expanded. Or at the very least, we now know where to set our default values! This is good news of a sort because it can simplify content generation. The shading system can now handle the Fresnel effect almost entirely on its own; it has only to consult some of the other pre-existing material properties, such as gloss and reflectivity.

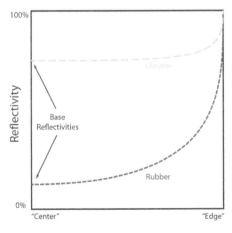

A PBR workflow has the artist specify, by one means or another, a 'base reflectivity'. This provides the minimum amount and colour of light reflected. The Fresnel effect, once rendered, will add reflectivity on top of the artist specified value, reaching up to 100% (white) at glancing angles. Essentially, the content describes the base and Fresnel's equations take over from there, making the surface more reflective at various angles as needed.

There is one big caveat for the Fresnel effect – it quickly becomes less evident as surfaces become less smooth. More information on this interaction will be given a bit later.

2.7 MICROSURFACE

The above descriptions of reflection and diffusion both depend on the orientation of the surface. On a large scale, this is supplied by the shape of the mesh being rendered, which may also make use of a normal map to describe smaller details. With this information, any rendering system can go to town, rendering diffusion and reflection quite well.

However, there is one big piece still missing. Most real-world surfaces have very small imperfections: tiny grooves, cracks, and lumps too little for the eye to see, and much too small to represent in a normal map of any sane resolution. Despite being invisible to the naked eye, these microscopic features affect the diffusion and reflection of light.

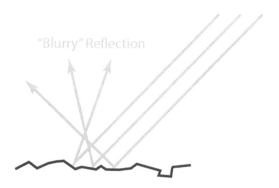

Microsurface detail has the most noticeable effect on reflection (subsurface diffusion is not greatly affected and will not be discussed further here). In the diagram above, you can see that parallel lines of incoming light begin to diverge when reflected from a rougher surface, as each ray hits a part of the surface with a different orientation. The analogue in the ball/wall analogy would be a cliffside or something similarly uneven: the ball is still going to bounce off but at an unpredictable angle. In short, the rougher the surface gets, the more the reflected light will diverge or appear 'blurry'.

Unfortunately, evaluating each Microsurface feature for shading would be prohibitive in terms of art production, memory use and computation. So, what are we to do? It turns out that if we give up on describing Microsurface detail directly and instead specify a general measure of roughness, we can write accurate shaders that produce similar results. This measure is often referred to as 'Gloss', 'Smoothness' or 'Roughness'. It can be specified as a texture or as a constant for a given material.

This Microsurface detail is a very important characteristic for any material, as the real world is full of a wide variety of Microsurface features. Gloss mapping is not a new concept, but it does play a pivotal role in physically-based shading since Microsurface detail has such a big effect on light reflection. As we will soon see, there are several considerations relating to Microsurface properties that a PBR shading system improves upon.

2.8 ENERGY CONSERVATION (AGAIN)

As our hypothetical shading system is now taking the Microsurface detail into account, and spreading reflected light appropriately, it must take care to reflect the correct amount of light. Regrettably, many older rendering systems got this wrong, reflecting too much or too little light, depending on the Microsurface roughness.

When the equations are properly balanced, a renderer should display rough surfaces as having larger reflection highlights, which appear dimmer than the smaller, sharper highlights of a smooth surface. It is this apparent difference in brightness that is key: both materials are reflecting the same amount of light, but the rougher surface is spreading it out in different directions, whereas the smoother surface is reflecting a more concentrated 'beam':

Increasing Gloss
(Constant Reflectivity)

Here we have a second form of energy conservation that must be maintained, in addition to the diffusion/reflection balance described earlier. Getting this right is one of the more important points required for any renderer aspiring to be 'physically-based'.

Further, an investigation of real-world materials will show that reflectivity values do not vary widely. A good example would be water and mud: both have very similar reflectivity, but since mud is quite rough and the surface of a puddle is very smooth, they appear very different in terms of their reflections. An artist creating such a scene in a PBR system would author the difference primarily through gloss or roughness maps rather than adjusting reflectivity, as shown below.

Microsurface properties have other subtle effects on reflection as well. For example, the 'edges-are-brighter' Fresnel effect diminishes somewhat with rougher surfaces (the chaotic nature of a rough surface 'scatters' the Fresnel effect, preventing the viewer from being able to clearly resolve it). Furthermore, large or concave Microsurface features can 'trap' light – causing it to reflect against the surface multiple times, increasing absorption and reducing brightness. Different rendering systems handle these details in different ways and to different extents, but the broad trend of rougher surfaces appearing dimmer is the same.

The previous one was adapted from the 'Basic Theory of Physically-Based Rendering' by Jeff Russell (https://marmoset.co/posts/basic-theory-of-physically-based-rendering/) (used with permission.)

CHAPTER 3

A Deeper Look into PBR

3.1 A DEEPER LOOK INTO PBR (PHYSICALLY-BASED RENDERING)

3.2 What Is Physically-Based Rendering?

Physically-based rendering (PBR) is a more up-to-date and in-depth rendering system in the game and cinema industry.

PBR calculates the LUX values from a sunlight source, calculates the shadow information from shadow cascades, and produces a more accurate and realistic world lighting scenario than its predecessor.

3.3 WHY DO WE USE PBR?

PBR allows us to have a consistent, realistic look throughout entire levels/ environments and worlds by using mathematical calculations even in different lighting circumstances. Although some environments will give a finished PBR Material/Asset a different look, it will always stay consistent with scientific parameters calculated via PBR workflows.

By using PBR, we eliminate the need to have texture maps that hold shadow and/or highlight information.

This means that we can create entire worlds with the ability to immediately change the lighting scenario and not have to re-render any information.

Here you can see how; by having a consistent PBR workflow, although none of the colours of our asset changes, the environment produces different looking aesthetics to the model. This is because light is being

DOI: 10.1201/9781003147497-3

calculated to produce a more natural, realistic look as it would in a real-world scenario.

- **Forest Environment:** You can see how the surrounding environment alters the look of the final weapon.

- **Sunset Environment:** You can see how the surrounding environment alters the look of the final weapon.

- **Sunrise:** You can see how the surrounding environment alters the look of the final weapon.

3.4 MATERIAL AESTHETICS

- An albedo, also known as a base colour (colour), is the physical property of the surface (ratio of incoming light reflected diffusely).

- An albedo is the colour of a material/surface.

- Derived from real-world measurements.

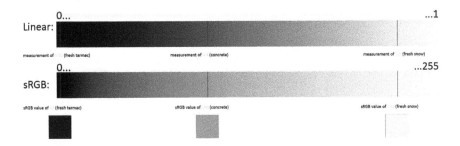

3.5 WHAT IS sRGB?

sRGB (Standard Red Green Blue) also defines a nonlinear transfer function between the intensity of these primaries and the actual number stored.

The curve is similar to the gamma response of a CRT display. This nonlinear conversion means that sRGB is a reasonably efficient use of the values in an integer-based image file to display human-discernible light levels.

Unlike most other RGB (Red, Green, Blue) colour spaces, the sRGB gamma cannot be expressed as a single numerical value.

The overall gamma is approximately 2.2, consisting of a linear (gamma 1.0) section near black and a nonlinear section elsewhere involving a 2.4 exponent and a gamma (slope of log output versus log input) changing from 1.0 through about 2.3. The purpose of the linear section is to prevent the curve to have an infinite slope at zero, which could cause numerical problems.

In the early days of the film and game industry's transition from chemical film to digital imaging, there was often confusion with the term 'linear' being used for all non-log-encoded data formats. Linear has a specific meaning, particularly in the areas of image compositing where linear often implies that there is a 1:1 relationship between the image data and light. Using the term gamma to differentiate video or other TRC-encoded imagery dates back to early television and broadcast engineering and is an appropriate way to define the different encoding types. Even if the actual TRC uses a piecewise curve such as the OETF of Rec709 or sRGB, one can still refer to it per the 'effective gamma'.

Scientifically speaking, every single thing on this planet emits an albedo (a colour).

You have to imagine that the world we live in does not have any shadow or lighting information.

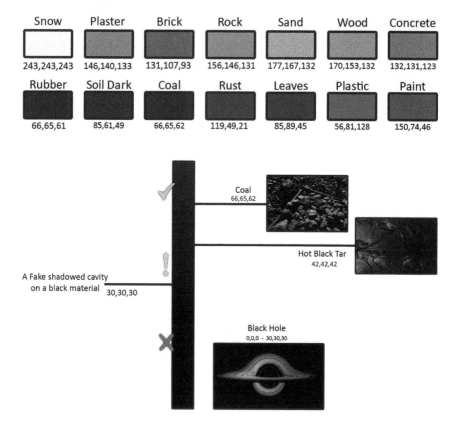

The basic principle is that if we remove the lighting and shadow information from any texture information, we can reproduce exactly the same results by re-lighting the environment, which allows us to change the direction of lighting inside of an environment without having to render the entire scene again.

The 'older' method to create realistic environments in the game and cinema industry was outdated, where we had to have 'shadow' information on our textures. The above images result in the same principle with a PBR material. The albedo (previously known as a diffuse) has no shadow or highlight information whatsoever.

Below are some scientific and also accurate colour samples/swatches of real-world assets and foliage.

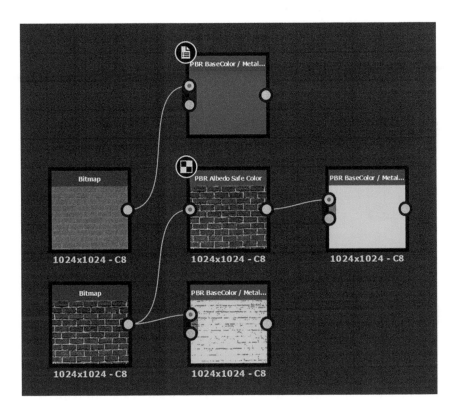

And now we will also look at correct colour values using real-work albedo values.

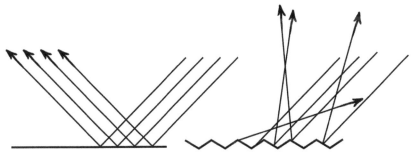

Smooth Surface   Rough Surface

When looking at this information, keep in mind that snow can never be absolute white; if snow would be absolute white, then you would not be able to see the reflections or highlights.

Coal could not be absolute black, because if it were, you would not be able to see the shape of the shadows.

When creating albedo values in the darker region, you must stick with the rules of PBR to achieve great realistic results.

If you create an albedo that is too dark, you will not be able to see the shadow information on the surface.

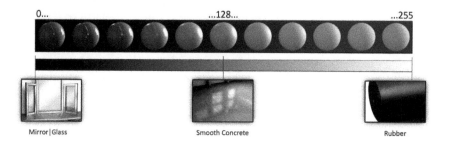

The best albedo tools can be found all over the Internet; however, you can also use tools within Photoshop and Substance Designer that already exist.

3.6 SUBSTANCE DESIGNER: PBR VALIDATE

3.6.1 How It Works

The PBR Validate tests between the ranges of 30sRGB and 50sRGB.

If the shadows are too dark or too light in a texture, the PBR Validate will show as RED instead of GREEN.

Any albedo found to be in the wrong colour range can be rectified by using PBR Albedo Safe Colour.

This will push the darker values lighter and the lighter values darker resulting in correct PBR values.

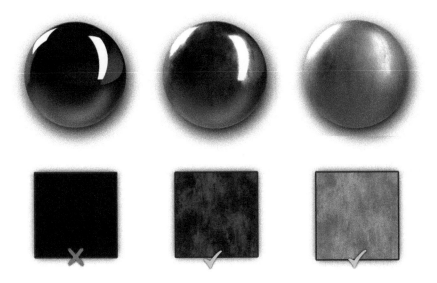

3.7 WHAT IS ROUGHNESS?

Roughness is a display of how smooth or rough the microscopic surface of a material is (too small to fit into a normal map). It displays whether or not the smoother or rougher surface will respond to light in the way a realistic surface would.

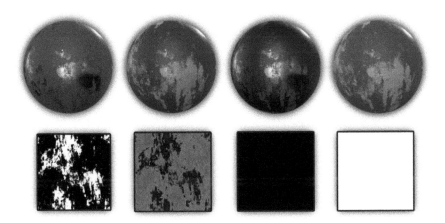

Gold	Chrome	Silver	Platinum	Copper	Iron	Titanium
255,220,157	225,225,225	250,249,255	214,209,200	251,216,184	192,189,186	206,200,194

There are numerous factors to take into consideration when creating the roughness amount on your surface.

What type of material is it? For instance, a mirror/glass type of surface would be closer toward the zero range giving a much smoother surface for light and the environment to bounce and reflect on.

Having just a single grayscale value for roughness maps will not result in appealing surface detail. To make surfaces look more realistic, there need to be minor 'tweaks' and variations to have a more natural look. Both light and dark roughness maps will achieve better results than a single grayscale colour.

3.8 WHAT IS METALLIC?

Metallic is one of the most important texture maps in a PBR material. Without a metallic map, metal surfaces would not appear as they would in a real-world environment and they would not reflect the correct values of the environment.

Electrically conductive materials, most notably metals, deserve a special mention at this point for a few reasons.

Firstly, they tend to be much more reflective than insulators (non-conductors). Conductors will usually exhibit reflectivities as high as 60%–90%, whereas insulators are generally much lower, in the 0%–20% range. These high reflectivities prevent most light from reaching the interior and scattering, giving metals a very 'shiny' look.

Secondly, reflectivity on conductors will sometimes vary across the visible spectrum, which means that their reflections appear tinted.

This colouring of reflection is rare even among conductors, but it does occur in some everyday materials (e.g. gold, copper and brass). Insulators as a general rule do not exhibit this effect, and their reflections are uncoloured.

Finally, electrical conductors will usually absorb rather than scatter any light that penetrates the surface.

This means that in theory, conductors will not show any evidence of diffuse light. In practice, however, there are often oxides or other residues on the surface of a metal that will scatter some small amounts of light.

It is this duality between metals and just about everything else that leads some rendering systems to adopt 'metalness' as a direct input.

In such systems, artists specify the degree to which a material behaves as a metal, rather than specifying only the albedo and reflectivity explicitly.

This is sometimes preferred as a simpler means of creating materials but is not necessarily a characteristic of PBR.

Using metallic on materials needs to be done correctly; for instance, mirrors and glass must have a metallic reflection to achieve better, more accurate results.

Metallic maps have to be perfectly made to achieve the best results. Below are four variations, each using different metallic texture maps.

When using metallic texture maps it is very important to stick within a range of Linear RGB 0 to 1, which means that 0 (Black) areas of a texture map tell the material/asset that any areas on the material/asset that show black texture/pixel information will respond to light as if it were NOT metallic.

Any areas on the material/asset that show white, tell the surface to respond as if it WERE metallic.

This can sometimes be very hard to differentiate. Sometimes artists will use the more sRGB 0–255 colour range for grayscale information, whilst this is acceptable again, sticking to a dark/light texture is key to achieving real results. As you can see, the Second PBR Ball has a lighter variation on the texture map, thus creating an unbelievable PBR-painted metal look. When you have two surfaces that transition between metal and non-metal, it is important to make the transition quick and precise, the moment the paint chips away, the underlayer is immediately METAL so should switch very quickly to white, not grey and then white.

Another important but often overlooked area of a metallic map is the albedo colour.

There are again strict rules to adhere to when creating metallic materials/assets.

Make sure that they often stick to these codes to result in the best visual representation.

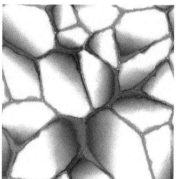

3.9 NORMAL TEXTURE MAP

The normal texture map is one of the most important textures to hold together a material, as you can see, the normal tells the surface to take a more complex shape adding surface detail and also telling how the light should respond and reflect from the surface.

Normal maps are **RGB** information on a texture map that stores 3D information corresponding to X, Y, and Z coordinates (hence, R, G and B).

Normal maps 'fake' small indents and bumps on a surface, the individual pixels include lighting calculations resulting in highlights and shadows that would be present if the geometry had more topology.

Now let us look at height texture maps.

3.10 HEIGHT TEXTURE MAP

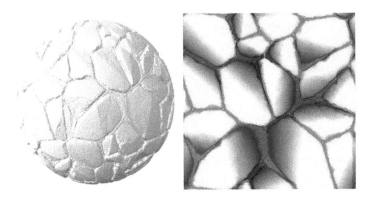

The Height Texture map, also known as the Displacement map or the Bump map, is also another important texture. Using grayscale information, we can 'fake' the offset of a surface using Height information. This again helps when you're creating a large scene and don't have the topology to support every tiny little detail like this rocky surface. Instead, we fake its height using a grayscale texture that uses 0 – 255 in black and white.

What does 0 – 255 mean?

0 – 255 is a colour range; 0 being completely black and 255 being completely white. As we get higher from 0 we start to transition to a dark gray colour, then a medium gray, light gray and finally white.

Look at this Gradient below and see how 0 (Black) uses the entire spectrum all the way up to 255 (White).

Now let us look at Roughness maps, these are extremely important.

3.11 ROUGHNESS TEXTURE MAP

The roughness texture map is key in 'selling' the believability that a material is realistic; as you can see, the 'shininess' of this sphere is seen specifically by areas of the roughness texture map.

Again, it uses a similar technique using grayscale information; it tells the surface where to act shiny and where to act matte; black surfaces will be the shiniest, and white surfaces will be completely matte.

Using real-world materials, you can understand that surfaces respond differently in certain light and different types of materials have different luminosity/shiny values.

Now let us look at albedo texture maps.

3.12 ALBEDO TEXTURE MAP

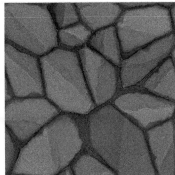

An albedo is the backbone of a material, as this is what holds the colour information on a surface. Using RGB channels, an albedo (also known as a base colour), can make our surface finally look finished.

An albedo is different from a diffuse texture as an albedo only holds colour information and does not hold highlights and shadows; however, to make a material look extra detailed, most material artists will usually have highlight values at around 20% and shadows at around 0.5%.

Diffuse texture will hold shadow and highlight information; however, this will also hinder the realistic detail as we can no longer have a dynamic lighting scenario to cast shadows onto the surface.

There are also metallic maps which use a 0–1 ratio black or white, and we can control whether or not a surface is metallic or a specific area that may also be metallic, but in this scenario, the rock should not have any metal so that all you would see a black texture.

CHAPTER 4

Substance Designer

4.1 SUBSTANCE DESIGNER

Substance Designer is a node-based, non-destructive application used for creating materials within the cinema and game industry. This node-based, non-destructive approach allows for easy adaption and alterations to materials, which in turn gives the creator the ability to allow for alterations between clients/studio higher-ups.

It also gives you the ability to view any created materials in real time, rendering visuals with environment global illumination and bounce lighting.

Overall, it is one of the industry's strongest tools and is a must for any artist who applies to gain employment in the industry these days.

4.2 UNDERSTANDING THE UI

Let us start by looking at our user interface of Substance Designer.

DOI: 10.1201/9781003147497-4

This is the screen you will most likely see at startup.

The first thing we are going to want to do is select.

File

then select

New Substance… (HotKey Ctrl+N)

You will then be greeted with this window:

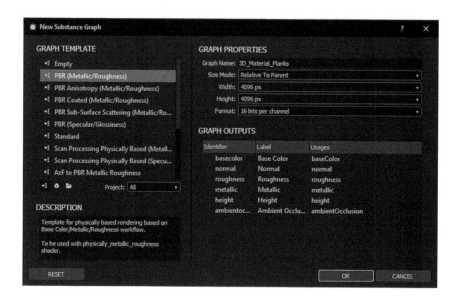

New Substance Graph

Make sure to select PBR (metallic/roughness) as this is the most used practice in the industry.

Next, let us name our graph which will be displayed in the Explorer Panel later on; for now, we are going to call our material/texture 'BrickWall'.

Now, we need to make sure that our size mode is set to Relative to Parent and not Absolute. (This will make it easier to change size at any time in the graph.)

Make sure to change the width and height to 2,048×2,048 to start with (this can be changed at any time without losing any information).

Once we are done, hit OK.

Now, we have our graph ready to start; here you can see all of our outputs on the right, and on the left are some default inputs that eventually we will replace.

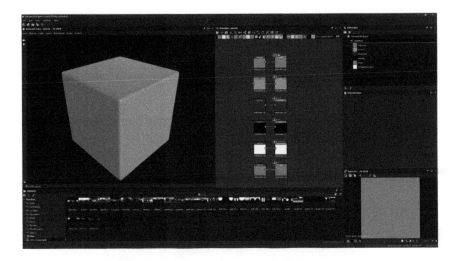

4.3 CREATING A BRICK WALL PATTERN

If you press the Space bar anywhere inside of the grid:

You can see a dropdown menu on the right, and this menu will allow you to select a wide range of different and most commonly used tools within the designer.

An alternative is using the bottom of the window where you will see Library.

What we are going to do is to type in the search 'tile generator'.

There are two types of tile generators: a colour version and a black-and-white version; for the majority of our work, we will mainly use black and white. Only use colour, when it comes to adding more colour information to our albedo map.

Left-click on our tile generator, and we will now have a new generator in our graph.

Now if you double-click on the tile generator, on the right side you will see this window.

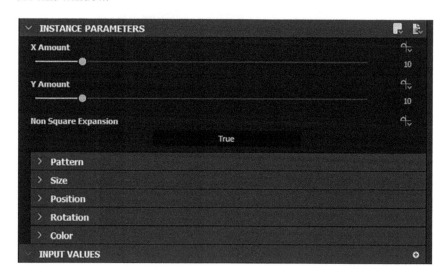

4.3.1 Instance Parameters

This is where you can start to change the shape and size of our brick pattern by using the buttons > Pattern > Size > Position > Rotation > Colour.

Let us start at the beginning and look more in-depth into size.

The main thing we need to change here is changing the pattern specific to 0, and this will leave us with no gaps whatsoever in our pattern.

There is a specific reason for this.

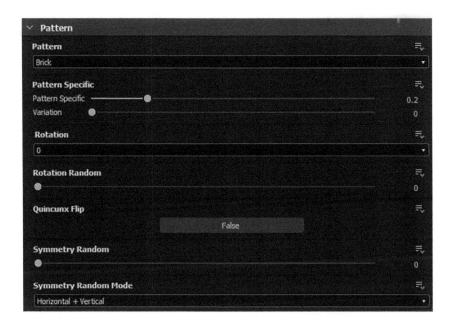

Now, we are going to go into Colour and change the Luminance Random all the way to 1:

If we have done this correctly, we will have a 2D view of this:

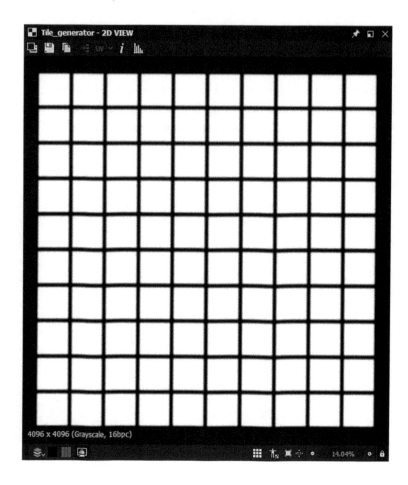

Now that we have this checkerboard pattern with random grayscale variations, we need to shape this more into a brick wall type: now, before going any further an important FACT that you should know is that ANY BRICK WALL before 1940 was built WITHOUT a CAVITY. So if you look at very old architectural buildings, you will notice different sizes of bricks as you can see on the image below on the left is a cavity wall. (These were built any time after the 1940s.) The idea behind the cavity wall is to leave a gap between the inner and exterior walls to put insulation inside of the house and keep heat in. Originally, this is started with polystyrene balls; however, modern techniques use wool or insulation boards.

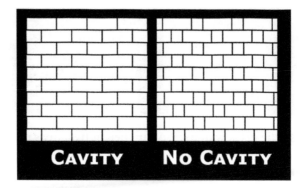

The first thing a great Environment Artist needs to know is what they want to do. For instance, when I was working on Sniper Elite and Zombie Army, the time period was 1939–1945 which means that if I want to sell the correct immersion, I need the environment to match the time scale, and creating no cavity walls would ensure that. So, knowing what time period or type of wall is one of the 'smaller' details that make a huge difference, and most junior artists often overlook this.

Now, instance parameters X and Y control the number of bricks.

The first mistake artists make is trying to 'replicate' brick scale in the real world. If you do this, you will lose a lot of information and will end up with blurry textures. However, if you wish to have more detail, you can create a smaller area of a brick wall and tile it (this will allow for much better detail).

If you wish to use the tiling technique to have more details, your X amount needs to be around 4 (this is the number of bricks across) and your Y amount needs to be 10 (the number of bricks up).

If you wish the brick wall to be of full height (usually 4 m), then double up the Y amount to 20 and X amount to 8.

(I would personally recommend using the tiling technique.)

Before you worry that the tiling technique will become absolute and cause issues, let me assure you when we finally get into using our textures in Unreal Engine you will see that you can blend multiple textures together to eliminate the tiling issues.

(Make sure that you change your Offset to 0.5 to have the brick pattern.)

Now, one thing very helpful when creating brick walls is having a good distance between the bricks and having a good mortar; to do this, we need to use a relatively new technique; for me, it was shown by a fellow teacher (Jordan Wills) at my university, where if you take an edge detect node and blend it with a blur node, you can control the 'bevel' of the brick in a uniform fashion:

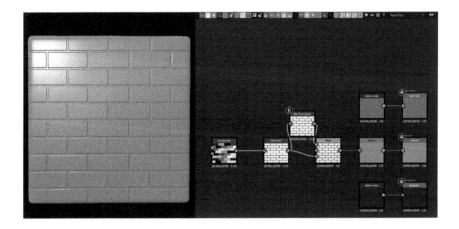

As you can see here, it gives you a nice result; just place the blend output node into a normal output like in the image above.

Whenever we create a material, the first two outputs we use most are the normal and height. This allows us to see how the shape and details would appear before we continue.

Personally, when I start, I also take an ambient occlusion from the final height output and adjust the levels and plug it into my base colour (albedo), which allows to see a little bit of shadow information quickly.

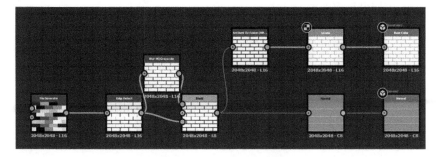

Before we go any further, the first thing I like to do is to keep my organization by adding comments to each section of my build-up as we continue to develop the process.

To do this, drag select the entire area and search for Frame using the space bar search.

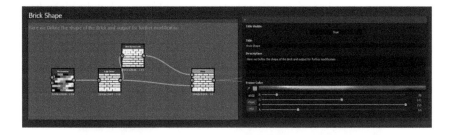

As you can see you can add more information to the right when you select it, and you can also colour coordinate all your frames (if that is what you like).

I recommend using frames always, because if you have to pass your work to another artist, it will be organized enough for them to understand your idea.

There have been times I have regretted doing this and having a messy graph.

Now we must also plug the output into the height map, and to see the difference though, we need to first click Materials in the 3D view window and select Default and go to Physically_metallic_roughness [Default] and choose Tessellation instead of Parallax Occlusion.

This will allow the height to be visible.

But to make the tessellation better, we have to change some settings again in Materials > Default > Edit >.

In the Settings for Height, the Scale should be at least 4 and the Tessellation factor 16.

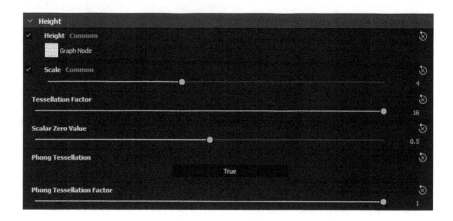

Now we should be able to see the height of the bricks in our 2D view, but to see that we need to connect our height output into our height input (this is usually a black-and-white image) for now, I am going to use the blend that we have set up.

Now we should be able to see the tessellation on our Rounded cube.

This will be our height, and it is always helpful to keep an eye on how 'realistic' it does or does not look so that we can adjust accordingly.

Now that we have our basic setup (Normal and Height), we can get to work on creating some really good detail.

You are first going to want to create the large brick damage (these are more protrusions and perforations).

If you blend the height output with a BnW Spots 2 node using a Subtract Blending mode, you should be able to create a nice 'noise' for the brick surface.

Then you are going to use a Slope Blur Grayscale (make sure that it is a Slope Blur Grayscale and not a slope blur) and use clouds 2 node to create the 'jagged' look on the brick surface.

After that, you are going to see the details 'pop' out.

A second Slope Blur Grayscale node can help you create more brick damage by using a Perlin noise.

(Both Slope Blur Grayscale nodes must have their mode set to 'Min'.)

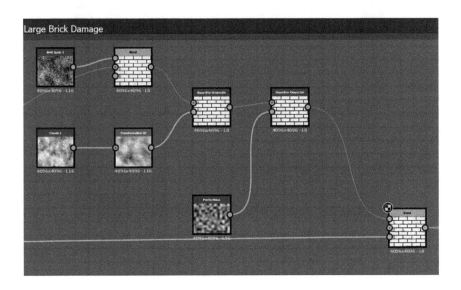

This is how the graph should look.

Now the key thing to remember when using Substance Designer for shapes is that:

Slope Blur Grayscale + Clouds = sharp Jagged cuts

Slope Blur Grayscale + Perlin Noise = Smooth slices

Another really good trick is to use a Slope Blur Grayscale on itself with a Blur HQGrayscale (this basically pushes the texel information around the area 'acting' like a Gaussian blur).

So as you can see, once you Slope Blur an image by its blurred self, you get some weird results, having a Histogram Scan will allow to select only the white points, spreading out the final textured dots. Using another Slope Blur Grayscale, I can now use the Clouds to give my 'dots' a jagged look.

Again, using the Blend node, I can subtract the damage and turn the opacity down resulting in a slightly worn brick.

Now, as you can see from this image below, we are starting to make this brick wall look a lot more realistic by adding small little grooves and indents and making sure that all the lines are NOT straight.

This is one thing to really take away when working as an Environment Artist, not only for materials but in general, making sure that nothing is ever STRAIGHT, having angels and damage and variation allows for a lot more story to be told.

When you see this brick wall, your first look is noticing that the bricks are slightly damaged, then you question; Why are they damaged? Did the builder accidentally chip away part of the brick when he was putting the wall up? Where they damaged during the transport? Has part of the wall fallen over the years causing part of this clay to become damaged?

It adds so much story and chaos for the eye to see.

Now that we are starting to get the hang of Substance Designer, we can step our game up a little. What we are going to do now is create the mortar for our brick.

Let us start by creating a Clouds 3 Node.

Now, if we use a Blur Grayscale with a quality set to 1 and intensity at around 5, we can use a Slope Blur Grayscale with the samples turned all the way up (32) and Intensity at around 2.5. Now, blend the Slope Blur with the original and change the blending mode to add (Linear Dodge), and this will now give us some high white values and a few low Grey values. Now, if we use a Dirt 1 and subtract it, we get this really cool Mortar Pattern.

This is also what the node should look like.

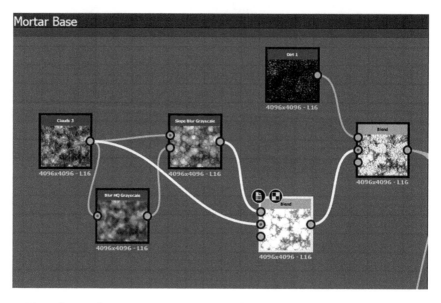

Now that we have our Mortar, we need to merge these two together, and one common tool that is often overlooked is the 'Height Blend' Tool.

Now, before we can go ahead and blend them, we need to set up a few things to help our cause; if we invert our Original Brick mask (so that the Mortar is white), we can use that as a mortar mask. However, we want our mortar to spread out a little more, and so we also need to create a blurred version we can push out.

If we blend our Mortar using the blurred Mortar Mask, we get some nice features. If we add a Clouds blend and use a Divide, we can brighten a few more areas, thus allowing us to pinpoint where the mortar can stick out further.

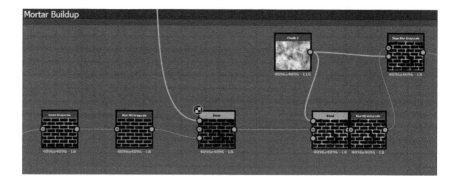

Now, all we need to do is to blend it with our brick.

Type in the spacebar and 'Height Blend' and use the Height Blend node. Here you will see two settings:

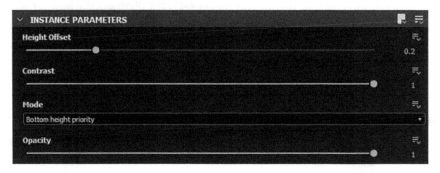

Play about with the settings. I find using a Histogram Range helps to balance the black-and-white areas out best. Below are my settings.

I use an ambient occlusion to detect the mortar shape from the brick, and then I invert the AO so that it is now black and white (white area will be the mortar mask). I then blur it, and push the white levels so that it covers more area. Then I use a clouds mask, blend that with the mortar and push a second histogram scan (or levels) to push the white levels, and then push that which now gives me a blurry mortar mask (this is helpful because blurring pushes the white outline further out of the mask area). Now, I use a slope blur to add a small extra detail, blend the mortar with the Final Mortar Mask, and then blend them together again with an overlay (this allows me to have whiter areas where the mortar is, and then plug it into the final height blend).

Here is the result:

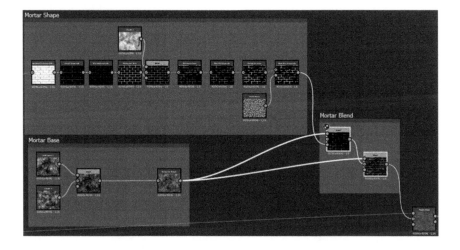

As you can see, by creating this shape correctly, I can add variation to the Brick Mortar. This is very helpful in adding story to your textures by giving the illusion that the mortar hasn't set right. Perhaps the builder was in a rush? Maybe over the years, it has become derelict or even a nuclear explosion has melted the mortar causing this build-up to happen.

The important detail to take away here is ALWAYS adding a story to whatever you are creating: whether it be a texture/material or even an entire environment.

Now that we have our shape, let us finish this substance designer demonstration by creating the albedo (this is another very important feature of realism within an environment).

There are several different ways artists create their albedo maps for their materials: they can use a blend with colours or they can use other methods. I prefer to take a curvature from my normal map; this allows me to gather normal/cavity and in-depth information of my model to create a detailed texture.

To start, let us create a curvature smooth node and use it on the output of the normal.

I also find it helpful to blend the curvature smooth output with a Fractal Sum or a noise and turn the opacity down.

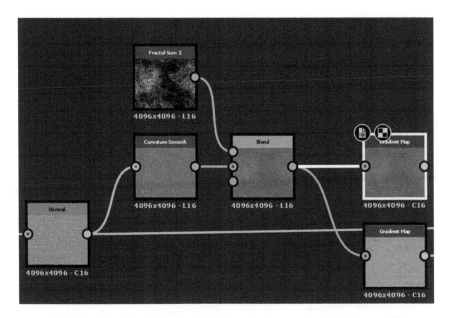

As you can see from the output here, it's greyscale still. Below is a gradient I've created to show you how you can pick a gradient in the Gradient Editor and pick colours. It's rather simple. Simply open a picture of a brick wall and left click and drag across the picture. The gradient will select multiple colours to use and add them into the various greyscale information we have.

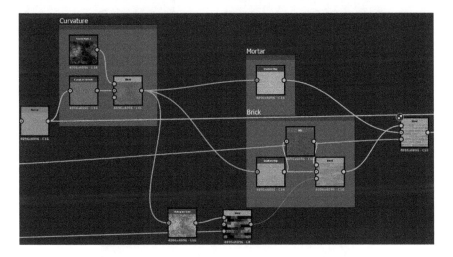

Now this is nowhere near finished, and we can add more variation to our texture by blending with several different masks; here you can see how the blend works and the final outcome.

I used the Height Blend Mask from the height blend for the Mortar and Brick colours to blend together.

All that is left to do now is to create a rough texture map from the albedo.

This is the final crucial part for storytelling in materials; without telling a correct story, the brick material will look bland. A simple grayscale conversion of our albedo will give us a base starting point. From there, we can make two copies of our grayscale conversion: one copy will be for the mortar, and the other copy will be for the brick.

Using a histogram range between the two blends will be crucial in real-time editing later down the line (this also makes our material less non-destructive).

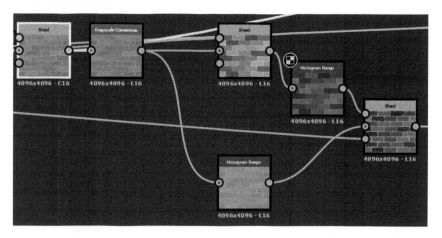

As you can see, I have blended the original random grayscale mask with the bricks and fed it into a blender with the mortar. Having a variation of brick values in grayscale will help make the brick more and less responsive to light depending on the value. Here is a final example:

Now that we have created a brick material inside Substance Designer, you should now be familiar with the process of creating a PBR material from nothing. If you have followed along correctly, not only will you have been able to create a PBR material, but you will now also understand the important of storytelling as an Environment Artist. Whilst this book is focusing on the importance of storytelling within creating materials, at most studios, it is very important that an Environment Artist can create their own materials for their levels. Having this skill is crucial to progress further in the industry as an Environment Artist.

Now we are going to look at another important skill that Environment Artists need: creating and understanding trim sheets.

To start, we are going to explore what trim sheets are, why they are used in the industry and how they can benefit you as a skilled Environment Artist. Then we will explore the process of creating a trim sheet within substance designer (again, a powerful, non-destructive tool that allows us to create materials in real time).

4.4 WHAT ARE TRIM SHEETS?

Trim sheets are a combination of multiple textures/materials for creating complex or even simple assets that use multiple different elements/materials within themselves.

Without using too much imagery, we are going to use our imagination.

Imagine a corridor. In that corridor, there are skirting boards, architrave, maybe even wooden wall panelling and, finally, wallpaper.

Now, each of these elements requires a single material, without packing our materials our average number of textures per material is 3.

Albedo Map – Normal Map – Roughness Map

That is if we do not have any fancy pants extras such as Emissive maps (if we are using a sci-fi level) and Opacity maps (tears in the wallpaper).

If we start to add up the amount of textures for these materials, we start to get more 'draw calls'. These are textures being called by the GPU to render. The more draw calls we have the more memory we are using. The more memory we use, the lower the frame rate will be. So, to rectify this, instead of using 12 textures for that corridor wall, we can add the wooden skirting board to the bottom of our trim sheet, and then add the architrave at the top of the trim sheet and the wood panelling in the middle. We could, of course, add the wallpaper too, but I find wallpaper easier if we use a tiling texture that we can alpha blend with a second version.

Now instead of using 12 textures, we are using only 6, and we have halved the number of draw calls used in this scene. A friend of mine had told me how in gears of war 4 they had a church, and the Environment Artist that was responsible for this church had created the entire church out of just trim sheets.

Trim sheets can be used for more than just interior spaces, and you can also use them on exterior spaces by putting a variation of bricks/plaster and tiles on exterior trim sheets.

Now we are going to set up a trim sheet specifically for an outdoor environment, and this will have a sidewalk, a small brick wall base and of course the curb.

Start fresh in Substance Designer and create a simple graph.

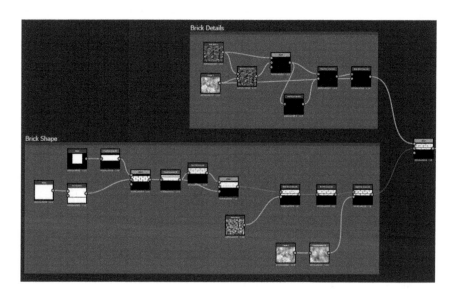

What you are looking at here is a simple shape connected to a transform 2D node. Now, when you connect the shape to the transform 2D node, you need to change one of the tiling settings so that it DOES NOT tile.

Under the Tiling mode, click on the little blue icon, and from the drop-down, choose 'Absolute', and this will now give you the ability to change tiling to No Tiling.

Now that we can change the tiling, we can use the little Lasso box inside our 2D view to change the scale of our size. We want to change the white area like so.

As you can see here on the right, we can change the scale to anything we want, and this is our best option as we need to make room for multiple different sizes and shapes for the entire trim sheet.

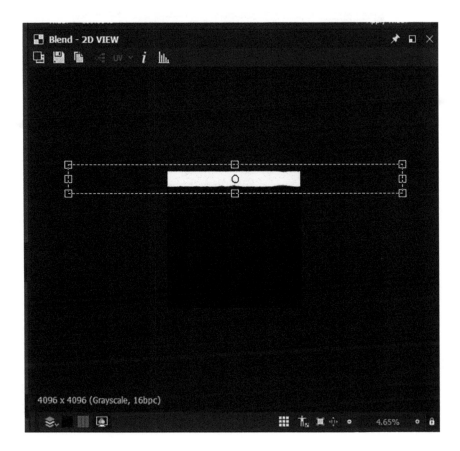

Once you have adjusted the shape, we will use a Slope Blur Grayscale with a Perlin noise.

Do not forget to change your Slope Blur Grayscale to:

Samples: 32

Intensity: Anywhere between 0.1 and 1

(when you blend a slope blur with a Perlin noise, it usually results in what looks like; broken/chipped parts off a floor/wall, etc.)

As you can see in the second picture, there are 'Chunks' missing out of the top 2 trims and a few bricks too.

This is how you achieve that result.

Once you have succeeded in creating this type of shape, you should add a second slope blur. This time, the slope blur; Slope should be a clouds 2 pattern.

The reason a clouds 2 pattern is good is that it adds chippings to the details we are trying to create before we created large chunks, but we want those large chunks to have damage. This is where the slope blur comes in handy.

For the curb details frame, start off with a BnW spots (anything that adds a variation of size and scale noise is a great thing to use here).

Again, use a slope blur to add some extra detail to the surface, and this is always good to have a variation in your images/patterns.

Blend two previous nodes into it and use a subtract, the idea here is we want to create the surface of the trim pieces, not the entire thing, so we can play with opacity to bring down the surface strength.

Once we have a surface detail we are happy with, there is a really good technique I like to use on surfaces to get some great small details. If you add your blend to both a slope blur and a blur at the same time, then slop blur them together, you get this really interesting effect that bubbles up your shape.

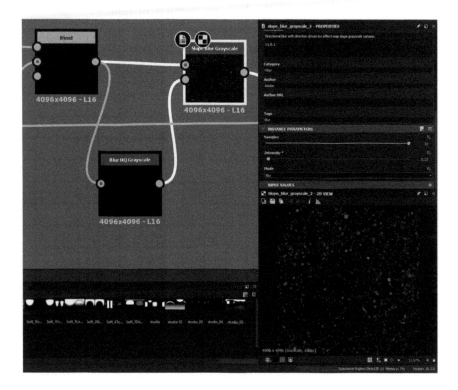

As you can see here, your BLUR will make your original input slightly different from the slope blur, thus 'stretching' the pixels digitally to create the interesting texture you see in the 2D view. This is a really great way to create asphalt.

In this instance, we do not want to create asphalt. So, if you add a second slope blur with a clouds 2 node, we can, again, break up the details slightly to get a better result.

Once you have your Curb Details and Curb Shape done, you can blend them together using a subtract in the blending mode.

If you copy and paste this and add some adjustments to the Transformation 2D, you can now tile the trim just underneath the first one, use a Blend node and set it to add (Linear Dodge).

This will overlay the other version on top.

Now, we move on to the Brick shape. Similar to how we created our previous shapes, we want to use a tile generator with a shape. The shape input/pattern input is easier to get a good brick shape than it is to create from just a tile generator.

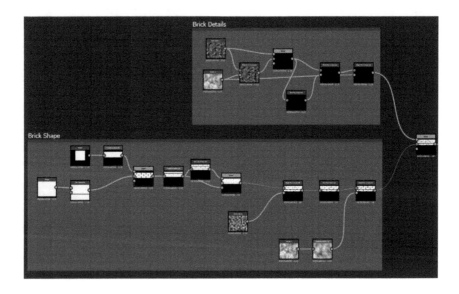

This is the same process as above. Eventually, you will have something that looks like the following image:

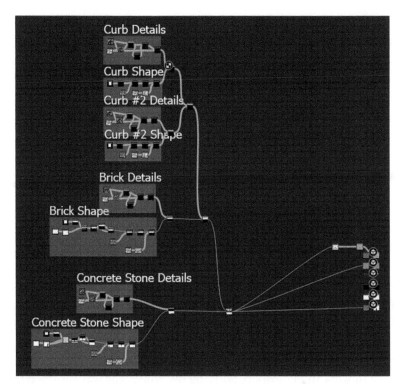

Here you can see how it should all link up. Again, approach texturing this the same way you would in the previous tutorial.

4.5 WHAT ABOUT FOLIAGE?

During the years I was working in the game industry, I have developed a knack/technique for working on foliage for games and cinematics. Along with other artists I have worked closely, I have realized that there are good and bad ways of making foliage; however, there are also fast and slow ways.

When I was working at Rebellion, I took it upon myself to build foliage libraries that consist of multiple variations of foliage: Summer, Autumn, Winter and Spring.

There was also a technique in which I preferred to work as I had worked closely with another artist who would use Photogrammetry techniques to re-create foliage.

What Is Photogrammetry?

Well, Photogrammetry is the art of taking multiple images of an object from different angles and then using those images inside programs such as Reality Capture, Agisoft Photoscan and 123D Catch (also other programs).

The program would then calculate the objects shape, surface volume and silhouette based on the pictures provided.

Few very interesting techniques can be used here to create the Perfect outcome, one of which I have used and learned from a friend of mine where you create the Entire 3D model from photos and then put the same photos into Photoshop and use the Camera Raw feature to remove the shadows and highlights, thus creating an albedo map. You can then re-run those images back through the software to create the texture too, and this makes great for realistic PBR settings.

But how does this work with foliage?

Well, my team and I once ventured into the woods near Oxford where we took a nifty little blue sheet. We put any foliage we wanted to scan (leaves, fronds, branches, etc.) on the blue sheet and took multiple images again to run through Photoscan software. This is where I got annoyed because it was taking too long, so I decided to do something different.

I took multiple pictures of different positions of the branches at high resolution, and then re-built them in Photoshop at massive resolutions (somewhere more than 32,000 by 32,000 pixels).

I then could have large detail to build my roughness maps, height maps and normal maps, but how could I build the maps good?

SUBSTANCE DESIGNER! That always worked well for me.

I got to work in Photoshop, building my atlases the way I wanted them:

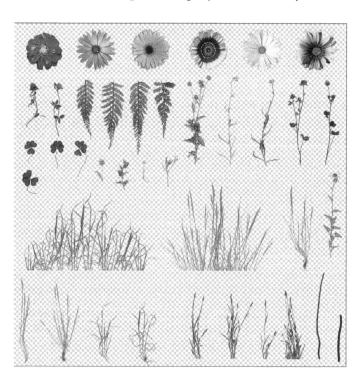

As per the image above, you can see how I decided to lay my atlas out. You may also ask, why would you lay your atlas out like this?

The answer is very simple.

Every object has 'draw calls', and these draw calls are the textures being ordered up by the GPU for visual reasons. If we create each of these atlases as single textures, we will have 39 individual textures. But wait, there is more!

Those textures would be materials because we would need more information such as opacity, translucency, normal and roughness.

So now we have five textures per material, and each object is its own material too, that is, now 39×5.

Forgive the mathematics lesson here, but now we are looking at 195 textures just for our ground cover. That is 195 Draw calls for our foliage. That may not seem like a lot, but when you think of an open world game using that many draw calls, we are also not taking into account trees, larger plants, terrains and more. It all adds up.

It all adds up.

So that is why building a ground cover atlas like this is very crucial and amazing for having high FPS and performance but using a lot of ground cover.

By putting all 39 objects onto a single image, we are not using only one material for all our ground cover. This, in return, gives us just five draw calls for our entire ground cover.

This means that we can use more of that ground cover too!

Knowing when to minimalize or reduce the number of textures/materials on an object to increase performance is a very important skill to have as an Environment Artist.

This makes you very desirable to game studios as not only can you create a good-looking foliage, but you can also create good-looking foliage that runs smoothly on multiple platforms because you know how to optimize it properly.

Now if I show you an image of a video from Unreal Engine's training on YouTube, they are explaining how foliage density is bad. However, if set up correctly and not overly complex, we have something that is still very good.

As you can see from the previous image, at the bottom there is a bar that shows what is good or bad: green is good, red is worse, and white is terrible.

Here is a Render from a small test scene.

You can see the field, and I have also cut off some of the complexity so that you can see how well it performs considering its density.

So, how do we do it?

Easy enough, just make sure to use all the experience and knowledge you have for substance designer. If you do not have any, our first exercise should be enough.

First, you are going to import two bitmap images: your albedo and your opacity.

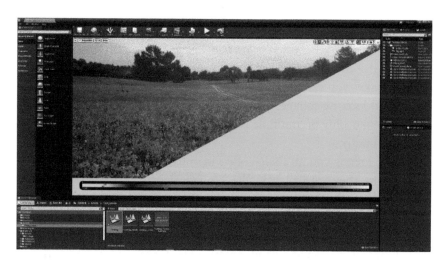

It should look something like the above.

If you have not got that Far yet let us start from the beginning.

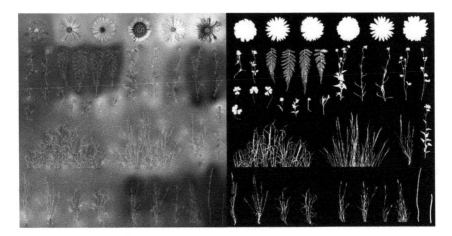

Firstly, lay out your atlas in Photoshop using the power of ×2, i.e. 2,048×2,048 or 4,096×4,096.

Then, we can start to create the albedo, and the next step is to blur a duplicate of the foliage from behind. The more we blur, the better the background will look (like above).

Merge your foliage together without the background (select all foliage pieces and press Control+E).

Now, duplicate a copy of your foliage (Control+J).

Move your duplicate under your original in the layers tab, and with it selected, go to Filter>Blur>Gaussian Blur.

In the Gaussian Blur settings, do something small at first like 3. So, now we should have our original foliage texture (all merged into one) and our duplicate blurred to a value of 3.

Now we can duplicate this layer three times and merge them together (the same way we merged our foliage). We want to keep our foliage separate so that we can use this as a final opacity mask.

Once you have duplicated the layers and merged, we are going to keep repeating this process over and over again. So: Duplicate three times, Merge together, Blur (now 6 instead of 3), Duplicate, Merge and repeat, doing 12 instead of 6. If we do this enough times, we can finally have our entire background merged to look like the above image.

Merge all layers apart from the original merged Layer, as we are going to use this as a mask. Duplicate a copy of your original Foliage and re-colour it white. Then, Merge it with a black blackground to create the Opacity mask.

If these steps are unclear and confusing (I think they probably are), there is a video I have created specifically for this demonstration: https://youtu.be/uUY1k7fxiQM.

You can watch the video on the link above.

So now that we have created our albedo and opacity, we can now import those into Substance Designer:

Right-click in the Graph and choose > Add Node > Bitmap

You are going to navigate to where you saved your Albedo map and Import it. Make sure to import resources, too, as Substance Designer will now use those resources to reference whenever you use this node.

You are then going to import a bitmap of the opacity too.

Now we are going to set up the entire process.

Similar to how we make our brick, we are going to use some cool techniques here.

Before we start using our albedo, we want to use our mask.

The process that I do is:

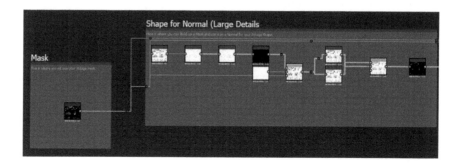

From the foliage mask, I link it to a normal and plug it into the normal output, and this will allow me to see the shape. From there, I can start to fine tune those details, and I start by inverting the normal map (you can use an invert node). This allows me to get the ambient occlusion from the shape. This ambient occlusion is crucial as this gives the foliage a 'feel' of it being more 3D through normal map manipulation.

I then take that ambient occlusion and blur using a Blur HQ Grayscale where I give it a slight blur to push the shape more. I then blend that blur with a white background using the original mask as the mask input for the blend. This allows for me to have a background blended correctly too. I then blur two different sizes again and blend them back together using a Max Lighten. (This will allow two blurs to blend together giving more feathered edge blur to the texture.) I then invert the final blend and plug that into the normal, and this is now my 'large' details on my foliage.

From there, I take my albedo and use a Grayscale Conversion node to convert my RGB into grayscale, and this I can tweak to get more results from a normal (this time using close details).

This again allows for me to blend the normals together, giving me a very realistic look, similar to how you would get the same result from photo scanning. However, this is actually four times quicker than the Photoscan process.

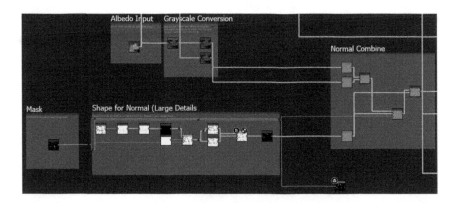

4.6 CREATING A ROCK MATERIAL

Another shape we can look at making is a Rock Material.

When setting up the Rock Material, make sure your outputs are high. I turn my normal map intensity up to about 15.

This is a lot easier than people make it out to be. We can start the process using a blank canvas and creating a shape node in the shape node settings. Make sure that you change the shape to 'Pyramid'. You can do this in the Instance Parameter settings and find 'Pattern'.

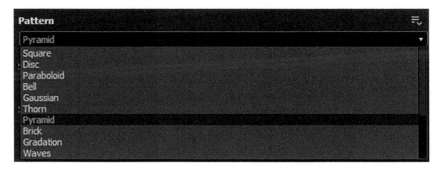

Add the shape node into the input of a Tile sampler node.

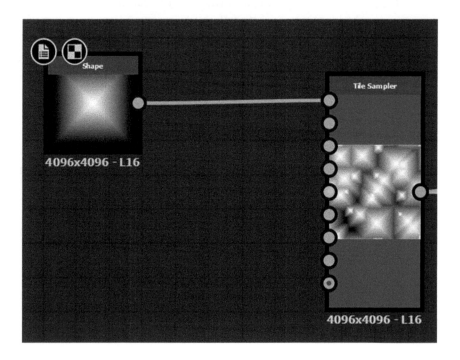

Using the Tile sampler node, we can sample multiple different inputs if needed. For now, we are just going to use the one input.

In the Tile Sampler, first, let us change the Pattern. Click on the drop-down and choose Pattern Input. Then we need to change X and Y amount to 5, and this will give us a larger area to work with.

Next, we need to change the scale. I have scaled my shape up to 3.21 in the scale and random at 0.88 to increase the variation.

We should also change the Position settings. Firstly, let us change the Position Random to 5.2, or just play with it slightly until you get a good feel for the shape.

Now usually you can create multiple different layers and use different grayscale values until you get a well-shaped height map for your rocks; however, you can easily do this with a 'Non-Uniform Direction Warp'.

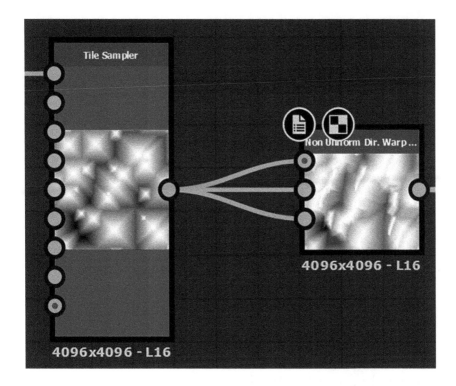

As you can see, from the Tile sampler to the non-uniform directional warp, we are starting to get more shape, and some of these settings are key to getting a good shape.

Let us look at the Instance Parameters.

Intensity controls the Intensity of the Warp. By default, it can only go up to 10. If you click on the number (on the right side of the slider), you can add a higher value. I often add around 100 and work backwards from there or forwards if need be.

For me, 68.25 worked well.

The warp angle controls the angle at which it will try to deform.

I turned my warp angle to −90°.

The Warp Angle Multiplier controls how strong the warp angle will be. This is not the overall intensity, but just the warp angle intensity. My Warp Angle Multiplier was set to 0.1, so the effect was not that strong.

Trail mode controls whether or not the direction warp will Max Lighten or Min Darken.

- Max Lighten will take all grayscale information and blend together to create a uniform gradient between low and high grayscale areas.

- Min Darken will take the grayscale information and invert the blend to create subtraction of the brighter areas.

- Average will take the grayscale information and somewhat Gaussian blur the shapes into a smoother grayscale map.

Depending on which of these you wish to use, each one of these will give you completely different results. So I suggest experimenting.

Trial length acts as an extrusion, pushing the values across instead of 'moving' the values across the screen.

Trail fade controls the backside of the extrusion on the mask, and it is always good to dive in to try these out and see visually what they do.

Trial curve controls the falloff between the grayscale values.

Here you can see the settings that I used to create my Rock Height map (Base).

It is always good to experiment with the settings to get a desired or even undesired but surprising effect.

Always keep your trial fade low, and you will get a lovely extrusion across the area.

Make sure you also plug your Tile sampler into your non-uniform directional warps:

- Input Setting

- Intensity Input

- Warp Angle Input

This will give you the best results.

Now we are going to add extra definition on top of our base height.

Create a Shadows node using our non-uniform directional warp as an input and let us find some shadow strength in our settings.

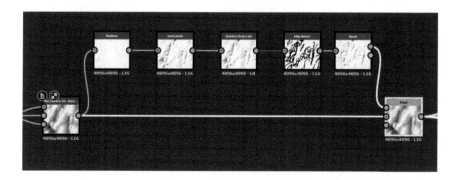

I have turned my shadow distance to 0.93 as I wanted to get some sort of shadow in the output. I created an auto levels node. Next, using the Shadow input, this will automatically darken the shadows more if needed.

Now I added a quantized grayscale (this is a very interesting node). If you ever work with stylized materials, using a quantised grayscale is a great way to select the colour palette. The quantized grayscale will take your entire 0–1 grayscale and break it down into bits. Similar to how you get stepping from low bitmap images, you can control the smoothness of the gradient by lowering the quantize. The lower the setting, the sharper the transition between dark and light images.

I set my quantize to 9 and added an edge detect.

Edge Detect is another great node that allows you to take grayscale gradients and break the shapes down into sharp-shaped images.

I used an edge width of 1.99 and an edge roundness of 0.24.

The edge width will give you great control over how big the cavity is in the edges, and the roundness will control the smoothness of the corners.

I added a Bevel after the edge detect to soften the edges furthermore.

In the Bevel, I gave a distance value of 0.07 and turned the smoothing all the way to 0.

Now, using a Blend mode and setting the Blending mode to Multiply, I can add additional edging to the height map, giving it a further look of sharp rocky edges.

I tuned the opacity down to 0.14 as I did not want a sharp look but only to add further detail.

To add even more 'Rock-Like' detail to your height, you can add a Slope Blur Grayscale node between your Bevel and the Blend node.

I added Clouds 2 as my slope and changed the samples to 32 and intensity to 0.5. I also changed the mode to min so that it cuts away at the shape instead of adding to it.

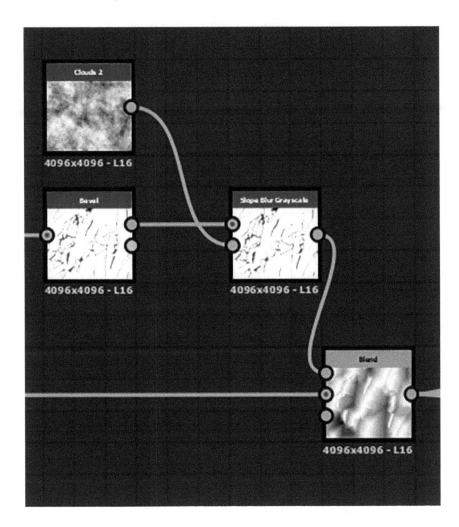

Before we go any further, I want to address some errors you may be getting.

So do not be afraid.

My normal map currently looks like this:

If you look closely at it you can see something called 'Stepping Artefacts'.

This means is that the grayscale information being fed into the normal map is not at a high-enough resolution to have a good sample ratio.

This is something I often point out to people who like to use TGA (Targa) as a source file.

If you use TGA and are saving a normal, it will become compressed at 8-Bit which will give you stepping artefacts. You have to save at 32 bits. Sometimes 16 bits works but will still give you errors on your normal map.

To fix this, you need to change your output format on every single node you make (sometimes it will take a parent, but that hardly works).

As you can see here:

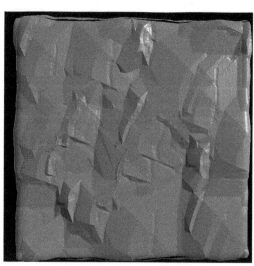

Even our geometry is showing the artefacts from the normal map.

To fix this, simply go to our base parameters and change the output format from 8 to 16 bits per channel.

If it is greyed-out, you just need to click on the little icon and change it from relative to input to absolute:

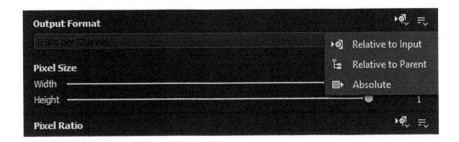

Now I will do the same thing again, and I will use a non-uniform directional warp except this time. I will use a Clouds 2 Node as my Warp Angle Input.

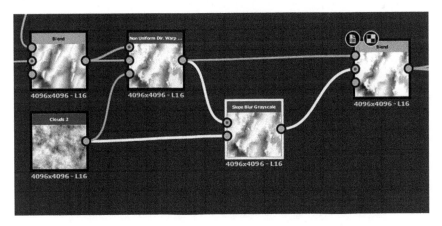

I will also use another slope blur and do the same thing again, use the Clouds 2 node and change the Blending mode to Min.

I also used a Blend node and blended my non-uniform directional warp and slope blur together, added Sub, and turned the Opacity down to 0.12.

This gave me some really nice rocky results.

Your material should look something like this now.

Now, I want to start adding finer details.

For this, I am going to use a BnW Spots 1 and a Dirt 4 Node.

I will add a Slope Blur Grayscale and ever so slightly adjust the slope blur intensity to 0.08. The blur mode is set to blur.

Then I will slope blur with a clouds 2 to add more cracks.

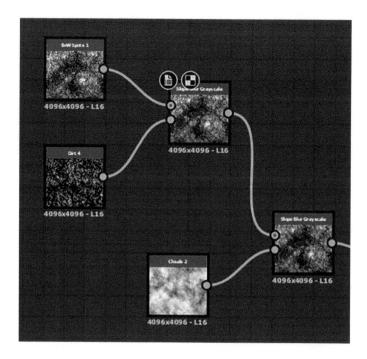

I blend this into the main Height map with an opacity of 0.05.

Blending mode is set to Min (Darken).

This will break the rock shape and give me some good perturbation so that the rock looks very jagged and weathered.

Now we can start to texture and add albedo colour to the rock for a more natural visual aid.

The easiest way I find a good starting point is by using the normal texture map as a foundation.

Add a 'Curvature Smooth' node to the Normal Map:

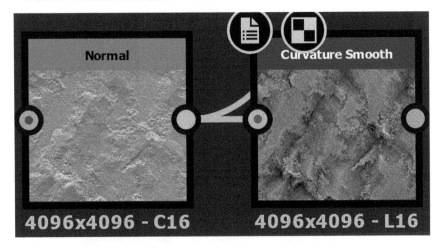

This will take all of your normal information and convert it to black-and-white information (this is not the same as height information, so do not use height).

We can take the curvature information that we have here and simply output a gradient map.

What you are looking for here is the Gradient Editor button on the bottom-right area of the Gradient Map Properties (see the image below).

Using the Gradient Editor, we can simply click on Pick Gradient.

Now, all we have to do is left-click and drag across any picture we want, and it will select a variety of colours.

I used this picture of a Mossy Rock side.

As you can see, the longer you hold and drag, the more colours the gradient editor will pick:

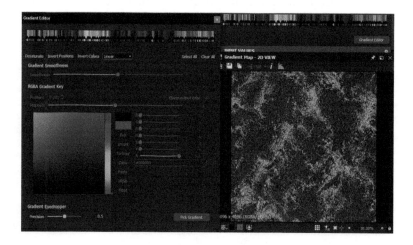

You can also select all and drag the slider to the left or right changing where the colours will be positioned on the texture map.

I did this several times until I was comfortable with what I had when I used my Curvature Smooth map as a mask to blend between one variation of the rock and another.

Then I will also blend an ambient occlusion over the top of my albedo (only at a low value so that it meets PBR standards), and finally, I will take a curvature from the normal and overlay the white values for sharper areas of the texture.

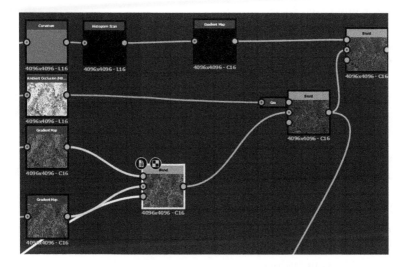

Now we have a nice-looking rock that has a moss growing on it:

We need to start working on the roughness.

This is one of the most important parts of a material because it could make or break the scene.

The easiest way is to take the colour information, and this will have albedo values and should already have somewhat of a value for how strong something should reflect light.

All we need to do then is to decide if the surface is smooth or rough.

I start by making a grayscale conversion of my final albedo output.

This will then feed into a levels node where I can adjust the strength of my dark and light values.

In this case, I want a medium range because some of my moss should be less shiny (moss does not tend to be very shiny).

However, some moss does.

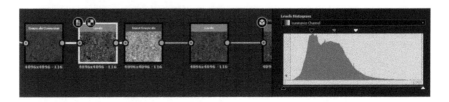

I take the dark and light values and push them into the middle and then invert that and add new levels. This will now control the overall amount of black or white values. Here, I will reduce them so that I do not get fully black or fully white values.

4.7 CREATING A 3D MATERIAL

Now we are going to look at how to create a 3D material.

A 3D material has multiple different layers inside it; for example, we are going to create a plank material that has joists and insulation underneath it.

Let us load a new scene in Substance Designer.

Make sure that when you create this material, we are going to change the Format to 16 bits per channel off the bat. This will ensure that our normals look flawless.

We are going to start with the joists for this.

Make sure that you change your scene object to a plane (Hi-Res) instead of a rounded cube. This way we will be able to see the detail as we work on it.

Let us start by creating a tile generator.

I will use a shape node and input a square shape.

I will change the X size to 0.29.

This will allow our tile generator to understand that there is black information there too.

In my tile generator, I will change the X amount to 5 and Y amount to 1.

Then, I will change the pattern type to Image Input.

Now, by default, the tile generator should slightly grey around the areas (similar to a blur), but we are going to push this grey value to white so that we have no tiling issues.

Plug our tile generator into a Histogram Scan. Histogram Scans are great for finding black-and-white areas and forcing the levels higher or lower.

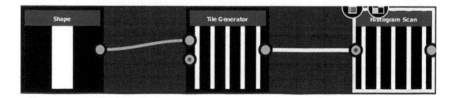

You should have something that looks like this.

By default, height is not enabled in our project, so we need to enable it: simply go to Materials > Default > physically_metallic_roughness [Default] and change it from Parallax Occlusion to Tessellation.

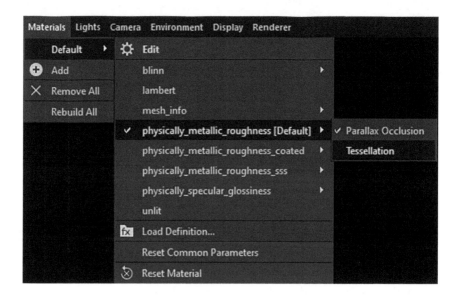

In our Properties tab on the right (once you select Materials > Edit), we can scroll down to see height:

Scale: 0 let us change this to 4

Tessellation Factor: Let us change this to 16

Now plug the Output into both a Normal map and a Height map.

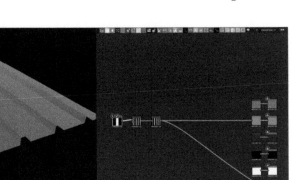

Now we can start working on the joist shape.

First, let us just change the shape of the joists as they are too wide currently.

In the Shape settings, we are going to change the X scale from 0.29 to 0.15 before we start adding more detail to the joist we are going to add the insulation.

If we take our joist shape information, we can use an ambient occlusion and invert the shading so that our darker values from the ambient occlusion is now our height information for the falloff of our insulation against the joists.

However, I prefer the falloff away from the joist as when you stuff insulation up together, it will bunch up more towards the middle:

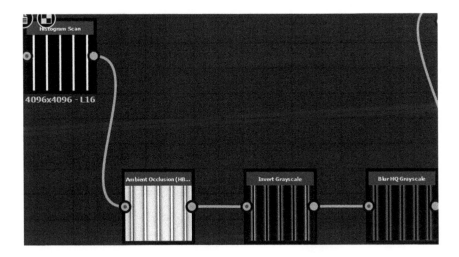

This is what it should look like.

If we blur the inverted map, we will get better results. Always use a Blur HQ Grayscale as within the Name. It is higher quality.

Now, here is where things could get lost in the text so I will supply imagery too.

Take the Histogram Scan and put it into the mask slot of a blend node. Also put it into the Foreground Input.

Take the Blur HQ Grayscale and put that in the background:

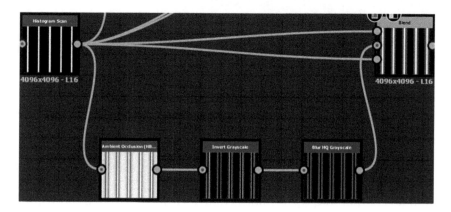

Now we can work on small larger details of our insulation.

We are going to create a Perlin noise.

My scale is set to 8, so it is not very high.

I will then feed the Perlin noise into both slots of a Slope Blur Grayscale.

This will take those shapes and push them closer together giving me a sharper Perlin noise.

Fun Fact: If you invert the Slope Blur Grayscale at this point, you can create water normals and caustics:

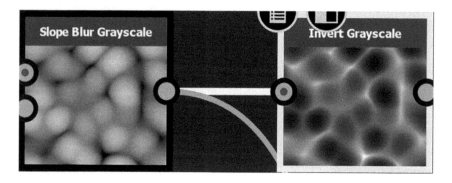

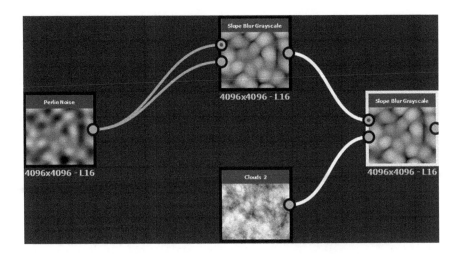

Now we are also going to use Clouds 2 with another Slope Blur Grayscale, This will chip away at the shape slightly.

If we take a Fractal Sum Base and a Clouds 2 Node and blend them with an Opacity value of 0.39, we can blend and go for some really nice noise on the insulation.

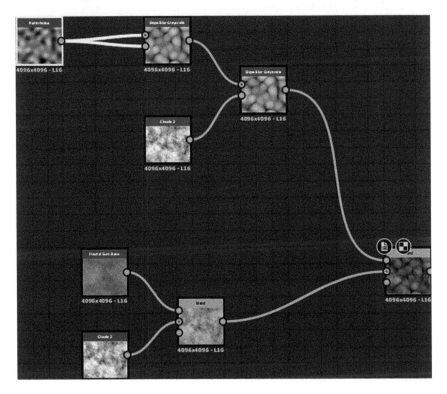

Now if we blend the two inputs together using the blend node, set your opacity to 0.95 (anywhere between 0.6 and 0.95 is good) and set your blending mode to multiply.

Now for the fun bit. If you Blend the Height Information of the Insulation Input with the Insulation Shape, you can make it even better by applying Bevel to the Joist Mask and Blend that with the final input. It will give you some really good normal details.

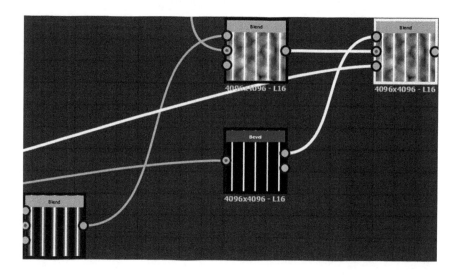

Let us just take a look and see where we are currently at.

Now we can add the small detail to the joists.

Let us start by using a direction noise.

The best way to create wood shapes is with directional warps, Perlin noise and directional noise (gradients can sometimes work too).

With a directional warp turn the intensity up to 255.

You will notice that our directional warp is a little crazy right now.

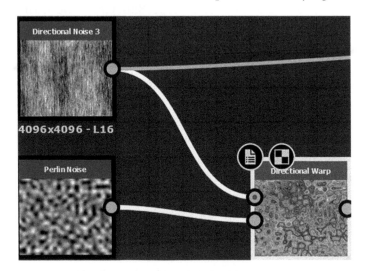

So what we are going to do is to use a Transform 2D Node and stretch it in the Y axis (height).

Change the height to 200% and press apply height. (You may have to do this twice.)

Once you have applied the height, the wood detail will start coming out:

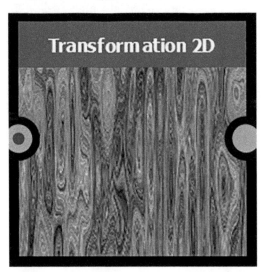

Use a Slope Blur Grayscale and input the Transformation 2D node into both slots. Make sure that the samples are up to 32 and the intensity is 0.02 (very low).

This will push the noise to be a little smoother.

Now use a Blur HQ Grayscale and turn the quality up and intensity to around 0.6.

Take the joist mask and use a Slope Blur Grayscale with a Perlin noise.

Turn the Slope Blur Intensity down to around 0.3 and samples up to 32.

This will create a 'chip' effect on the joists and make them a little more imperfect.

Blend the wood noise shape with the joists' imperfection. Now blend them again this time using the original directional noise.

Here is an image of how that part of the node should look.

If you have done this correctly, all you have to do is to blend both the joist and the insulation together and reduce the opacity down (make sure to use the joist mask so that you only replace the joist detail information).

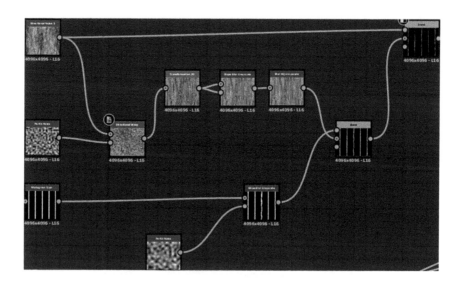

Now we are starting to get some great detail on the wood:

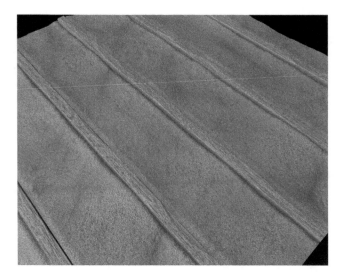

Before we start adding texture details, we need to finish by adding our boards, and that way we can mask everything out correctly.

First, we need to create a new shape node.

Input the shape node into the tile generator and input the tile generator into the Histogram Scan.

For our tile generator settings, we are going to use:

X Amount: 2, Y Amount: 12

Pattern: Image Input, change our Offset to 0.23 and we are good to go.

We will use a Histogram Scan to sort the bevelling out on our planks.

A really cool tool to use here is a Flood Fill.

The Flood Fill will find white areas and fill them with a variety of different additions: you can use Flood Fill to random grayscale, random colour, random size, etc.

Here is the really cool part.

If we use Flood Fill to random grayscale, we can randomize the grayscale amount via seeding.

We can also use a histogram shift to allow randomization even further. Adding a final histogram Scan, we can turn up the Contrast fully and the position anywhere we want. This will randomly select white values to add Planks (if we want a broken floor and to be able to see the underneath).

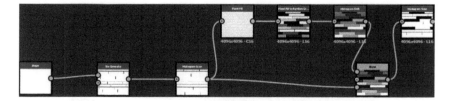

Here is another image of how it should look. I also used a blend node with a mask so that the background is black.

If you add a blend node using the Histogram Scan node as a mask, then you will get results like the image below:

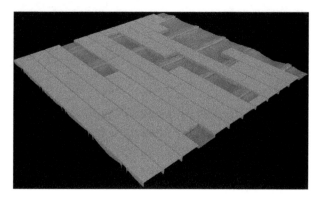

Here is how we are looking so far.

We are starting to make some good progression now.

You can play with the Histogram shift to see how the planks will procedurally generate on the surface.

Keep in mind that we are using height, so the planks will not be 3D object planks but 3D Height so they will drag down.

Now we need to do the last step in detailing our material by creating plank details.

Duplicate the wood details that we made and rotate the directional noise to 90°, stretch in the opposite direction in the Transformation 2D node and blend with another directional noise like:

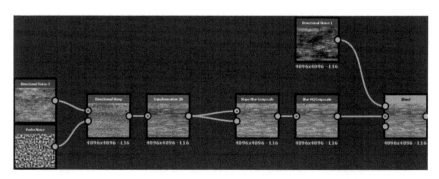

Use a blend node and use the Histogram Scan mask from your planks:

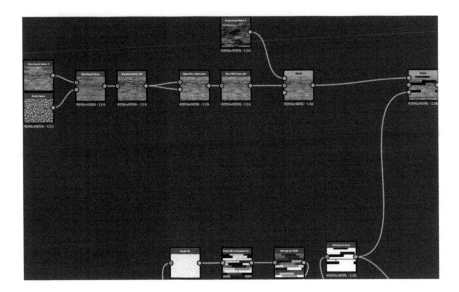

Make sure to use a Slope Blur Grayscale on the planks with a Perlin noise.

This will add some wear and tear to the planks so that they are not so uniformly straight.

Now we can use a levels node (as we are also using this for height, we want it to be mainly white).

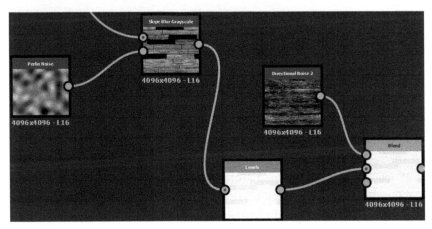

Blend again on top of our joist and insulation and now we have plank detail too.

Now we are starting to get the detail we want.

Let us look at texturing.

Here is where it gets messy.

First, take a Curvature Smooth node from the normal output:

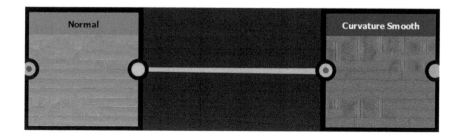

This will give us some smooth values that could work nicely when texturing the material.

Next, we are going to create three gradients: one will be for our insulation, one will be for our joists and one will be for our planks.

The best way to do this is by using Google and also the gradient map.

If we use a gradient map from our Curvature Smooth, we can use the Gradient Editor to pick some good colours and then Google search 'Insulation' to find a good picture. Then, simply use the Gradient Editor with a Pick Colour.

I actually used this twice and got my joist texture from the beams here.

Next, we need a planks texture, so we'll do the same thing. Google wood planks (I googled council flooring for this). Also, use HSL (Hue Saturation Lightness) if you want to do some extra tweaking.

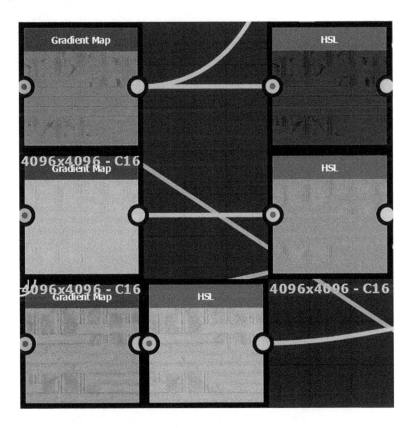

Even if I have not used the HSL, I still add them.

Now we need to work on the masks.

First, we need to use a blend node and subtract the planks mask from the joists mask.

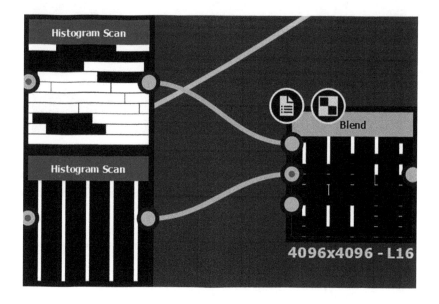

Using the subtract, we can have a blend node that allows us to blend both the joist and the insulation at once:

Then, we can blend the planks on top of that.

Before we blend our planks, we need to go through a rigorous process of adding more detail to the albedo.

We are going to make the wood detail as we did before, except this time we are going to use a Perlin noise and a directional warp.

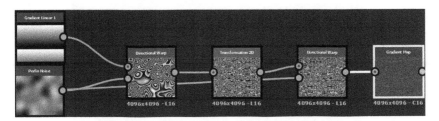

I always turn my directional warp up to something crazy like 2,000 or more.

This gives good results. I then use the Transformation 2D node to stretch in both the x and y directions and give me a more wood-like pattern.

I will use a blend node and reduce the opacity blending it over the wood gradient until I have a very subtle looking wood plank.

Here I will take a Histogram shift from the planks mask and use that as a mask on a blend node. Inside that blend node, we can use an HSL to change the look of our planks and overlay it with this grayscale. This allows us to have planks that have several different shades of colours. This makes them look more chaotic and not uniform.

By blending together using the planks mask, we now have our albedo done:

I often find that adding an ambient occlusion with a value of around 0.2 is good to add to an Albedo. This usually gives you a tiny little bit more detail.

Now that we have some good detail and a good starting point, we can work on the roughness map.

I am going to do the same thing with the roughness that I did for my albedo and use the masks to mask each area.

That way, I can control the roughness of my surface.

My insulation should hardly reflect any light, whereas my planks should reflect the environment and lighting a lot more.

As a bonus, you can also take the tile generator you have used for your planks and replace the shape with a cylinder (depending on how you make your planks, you may need to squash your cylinder):

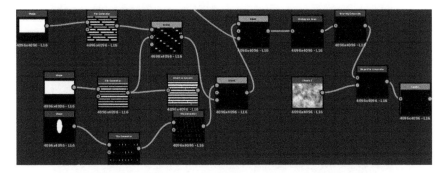

Here I used the planks in different orders to mask and subtract from each other, thus giving me specific areas for the nails to go. This will give me nails at the end of the planks like:

4.8 LAVA

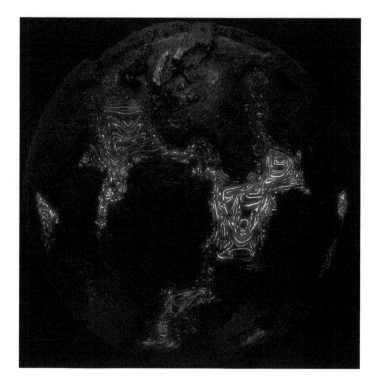

This is the material we are going to focus on making now.

And to make it even easier, we are going to use a material we have already made (the Rock tutorial).

If you have not tried making the Rock yet, now is the perfect time to dive in.

Once you have finished the Rock tutorial, save a copy and let us get started.

We are going to remove a lot of work and also tweak a lot of work here. So do not worry too much about the albedo for now.

First of all, take the Height Output (Slope Blur Grayscale), and we are going to blend it using a height blend.

Set up a Height Blend node that we can come back to once we are ready without lava.

Our goal here is to create something like this:

To create this kind of 'Blobby' lines, we need to create the base shape. I start with a BnW Spots 2 node and plug the output into a Blur HQ Grayscale node. I then plug it into a Slope Blur Grayscale and use the Blur HQ Grayscale node to blur the shape (this will allow us to use the Slope Blur Grayscale node to 'push' the shape out more):

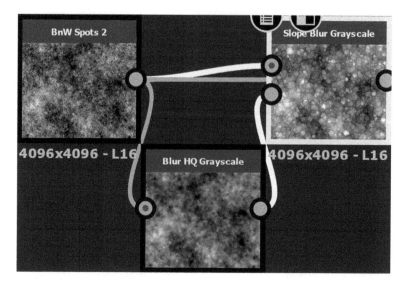

As you can see, now we have a good starting shape to progress from.

Now we need to create a blend node to blend our BnW Spots 2 and Slope Blur Grayscale Node together.

For my settings, I have changed my blending node to subtract. I have also kept my Opacity at 100. This will take the noise from the shape and leave us with a nice 'rocky' surface.

Now for those wiggly lines, we are going to start creating these lines by first using a directional warp. If we use a Perlin noise a second time, we can get some interesting shapes.

I will use a second directional warp again to push the shapes further. Do not forget to use crazy numbers for your intensity values. The idea is to push the shapes and make them swirl.

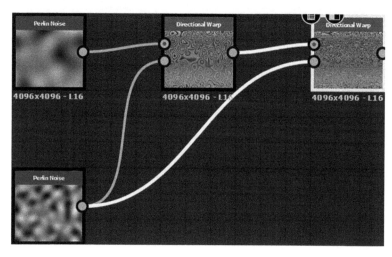

On my first directional warp, I set the intensity to 2,900 and on the second directional warp, I set it to 216.

This will give me the shape I want to re-create the lava look.

I will then create a blend node and blend the swirl shapes with the rocky surface we created using the BnW Spots 2 node.

Turn the opacity down to around 0.3 so that we can blend the noise over the swirls (this will give our lava some perforation but still keep the shape looking good).

I noticed here that my lava shape was a little too sharp, so I decided to give it another Slope Blur Grayscale and I used the same process. Using a Blur HQ Grayscale node, I managed to push the shape out more giving it a more liquefied look.

Then I used a directional warp and used my warp input as a Gradient Linear 1.

The black to white ratio allows me to push values in a specific direction: in this case, I wanted to push it up slightly.

I then blurred the height slightly using another Blur HQ Grayscale and then decided to use a levels node. Here I pushed the values to a good balance for blending with height. I chose a specific grey value which was where my lava would sit at a level base, and then I used the height blend:

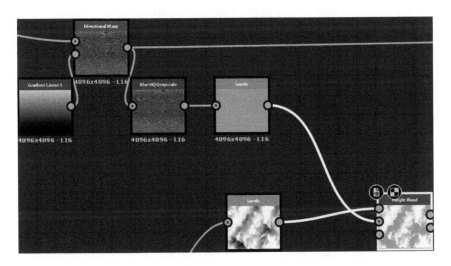

Here you can see the blending settings.

The levels on the bottom of this image is from our rock output and the levels on the top height blend is the levels from our lava output.

Height blends are a great way to blend multiple different layers together using the black and white information you have created.

Remember that when blending this height information close together, you should always use a levels node to control the height even further.

In my height blend node, I changed the height offset value to 0.52 and the contrast to 1. This allows for a sharp transition between the two heights.

I want to talk about the lava height levels.

It may look completely grey in this image, but believe it or not Substance Designer is a very powerful tool and it will notice the slightest variation between dark grey and a little bit darker than dark grey.

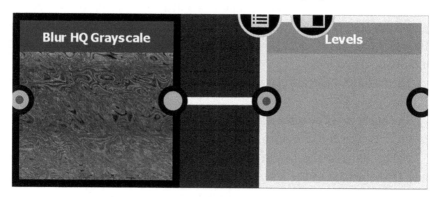

All we have done in this image is restrict how deep our height map will be. We want our swirly lava pattern to sit close to the base surface.

The next part of this process is madness, and you will probably find an easier way of doing it. However, during my trial-and-error phases, I just threw nodes all over the place until I get the outcome I am looking for.

From my height blend output, I will use the mask of the height blend to create an ambient occlusion. I will use this ambient occlusion to create the 'shape' of my lava area and use it to push the swirls even more.

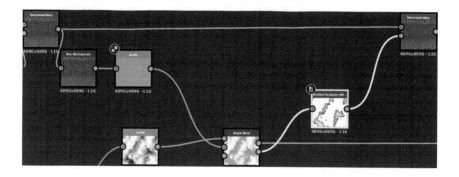

As you can see in this image, what I have done is use another directional warp, but this time instead of using a specific direction (anywhere inside of the lower valleys of the rock), using the ambient occlusion, I am telling the direction warp to push the swirls more using this specific direction and shape.

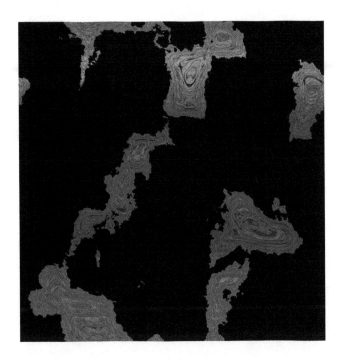

As you can see in this image, the swirls start to take on this shape (which is the area the lava will be).

I then put the shape through another blend node where I will use the rock shape I did earlier on (using the BnW Spots 2 node) and I will change the blending mode to add Sub and also reduce the opacity to around 0.16, and this will give me more of a rocky surface (in case I lost any of it earlier).

I will then put that output into the Blur HW Grayscale node where only slightly blur (I used a value of 0.33), and then I will put the Blur HQ Grayscale node into a blend node, blending a Perlin noise, I did this to add different height values to my shape a little more.

This is where the crazy bit is.

We have already used the height blend node. However, the height blend node gives us a mask as an output, and we could not use that mask output to get the ambient occlusion and blend it with itself, so instead, we had to take the mask output, do a little crazy maths to get the shape and push the lava swirls and then re-blend the height. Now, we can use our height blend in bottom input and the new levels that we just made in our top input.

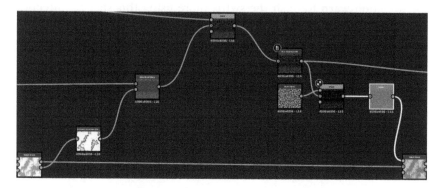

Hopefully, this node makes more sense than I am trying to make right here. Now to the texturing.

Before we start with the albedo, we need to create our lava mask.

I created a blend node and used the Height Blend Mask as my mask and left my background empty, and in the foreground, I used the lava shape I created. This allowed me to have a specific area for my lava ONLY to work with.

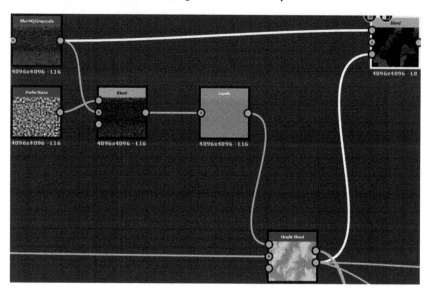

As you can see, the blend node (top right) only has information on where the lava will be, and the rest of it is black. This is very helpful for us because we only need this area to mask out.

Here we could potentially just invert the mask, so the darker areas are where the lava will be emitting from. However, it will not look good. So instead, I am going to put my blend node into an ambient occlusion input and then invert the ambient occlusion input to get my brighter areas.

For my ambient occlusion, I changed my height depth to 0.03 so that it was very small. I then inverted the ambient occlusion and used a levels node to push my whiter values higher. After that, I used a blend node with the Height Blend Mask and again the background was blank (So it stays black). My mask looks like:

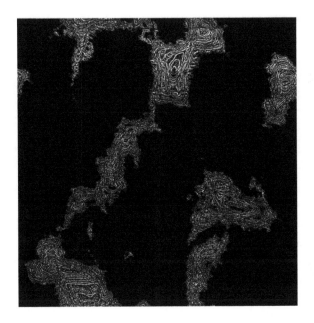

You can also see the node to make sure you are following correctly.

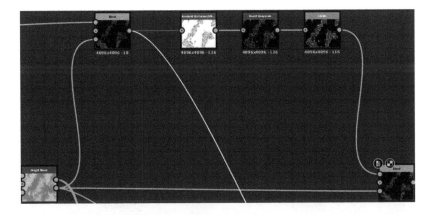

Now that we have this mask, we can start working on our albedo.

We are going to remove all our albedo from our previous rock (if you have it), and we are going to take a new Curvature Smooth node from our Normal output and create two new gradient maps.

One is going to be the rock surface and the other is going to be the lava surface.

Remember that an easy way of finding colours is to use Google and use the Pick Gradient button in the Gradient Map.

First I am going to use an HSL to add more saturation into my lava colours.

Then I will use a blend node to blend ONLY the lava area. For this, I am simply using that lava ambient occlusion node I made for the glow.

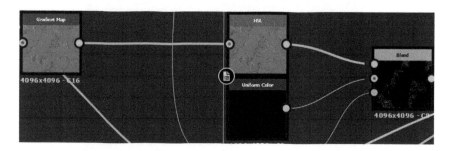

Once I have got my lava colour, I will then use another blend node to blend my lava with my rock. Using another blend node, I will use the Height Blend Mask as my mask for the blend node and put my rock into the background and lava into the foreground.

Again, using the albedo, we can convert this into grayscale information and tweak our values to get some good roughness on our surface. The next step is to add an output node into the scene (a new output node), and in the integration attributes, we want to click on Add Item and change the Usage (using the dropdown tab) to Emissive.

This may seem like confusing information, so again there is an image on the next page for how you can go about doing this.

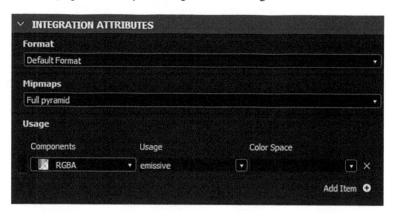

Once we have added our output, we need to right-click anywhere in the graph and choose View Output nodes in 3D.

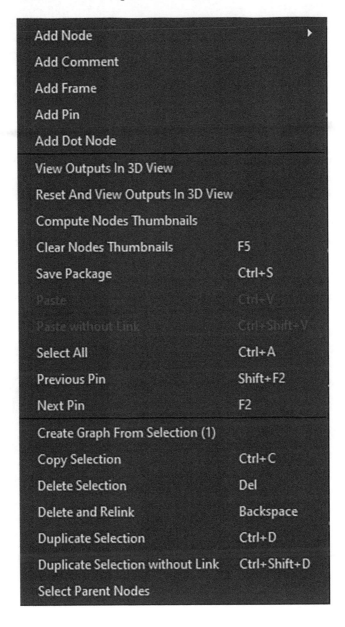

This will give us a new output to add our emissive map too.

Simply drag your blend node into the input of your emissive output and Jobs a gooden'

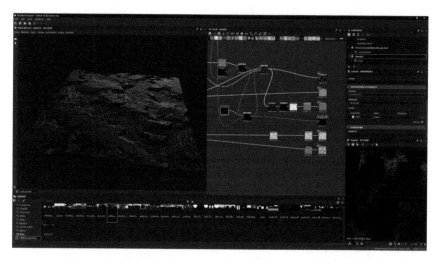

You will notice that in Substance Designer, you will not get the emissive values you are looking for. However, this is only because Substance Designers' emissive values are not great by default. There are two ways we can do this: either set up a scene in Marmoset or Unreal Engine or whatever program you are using to render 3D models, and make sure you have a bloom.

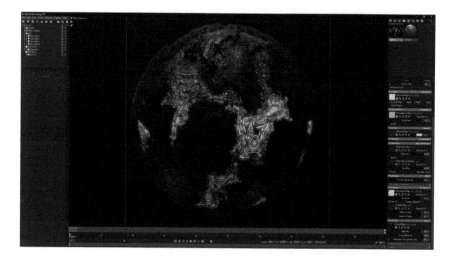

4.9 FABRIC

For our final designer tutorial, we are going to look at creating a simple fabric material.

This can be modified and used in a number of larger material sets, and you can also import these materials into Substance Painter and use them as a smart material for clothing.

To start, we are going to set up a new project and we are also going to keep in line with what we are doing by simply making sure our format is still using 16 bits per channel.

The first node we are going to use here is the Waveform Node Press Space in the graph and type in Waveform and we will use Waveform 1.

In the property settings, we need to change the:

SizeMin to 0.37

SizeMax to 0.54

WaveNumber to −1

Noise to −0

and the Pattern to 2

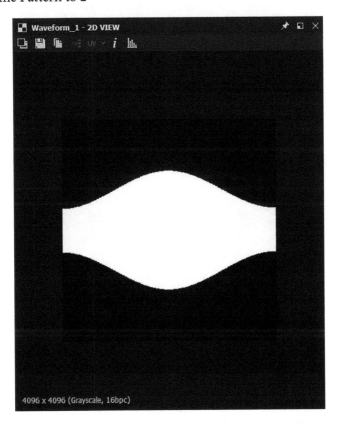

This will give us the shape we are going for in terms of woven fabric. Now we are going to add a shape node:

In the pattern properties, let us change the shape to hemisphere and we are also going to need a blend node.

Plug the Waveform into the blend node. Foreground and plug the hemisphere shape into the background node of the plugin.

Set the blend node to multiply, and this will give us some height to the strand.

The shape is a little sharp, so let us use a Blur HQ Grayscale and turn the intensity up to 16.

Add a levels node and move the mid-channel up to the right slightly. We only want to do this the smallest amount (basically to take the white areas away from the edges).

This is what you will want the shape to look like.

Now comes the real fun; we are going to use a Tiling Generator node to tile the pattern we have just created.

Plug the levels node into the tile generator input.

In the tile generator properties, change the pattern to image input.

Turn the X amount down to 5 and the Y amount to 1.

Scroll down to the bottom of the properties and change the blending mode to Max.

This will allow for our shapes to overwrite some height information but not completely replace it.

I am going to change my scale to 1.33 and my interstice Y to 0.24.

I will also change my rotation to 20°.

Any further changes needed we will come back to later, as we now need to set up the rest of this graph.

I am going to have two Transformations 2D nodes and set them up to have a blend node. Using the blending mode, we will use Max Lighten. At this point I will go back to my Transformation 2D node and change the Angle Rotation by 90 degrees.

I have moved one of my nodes slightly by using the offset or just by left-clicking anywhere in the 2D View and dragging.

This is what you should have so far.

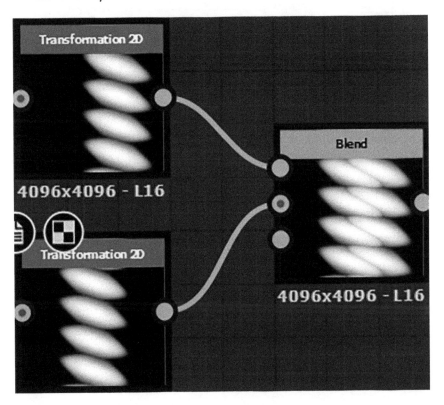

However, we want to create a V shape for the Fabric. So in my Second Transformation 2D node, I want to click on 'Vert Mirror', which will flip on one axis.

I will move that until I get a pattern like this:

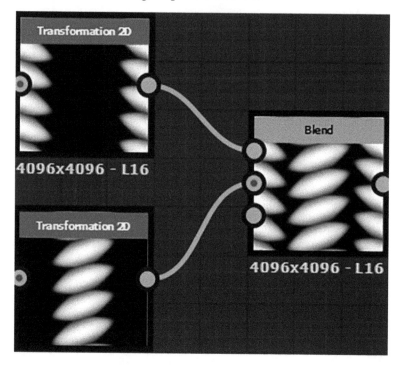

Now I will go back into the tile generator and will change the rotation to 61. Now, it should look like a rope pattern.

Then I will start to change my interstice Y again. First, I will set the interstice Y value to 0.51 and manually click on the Interstice X Number and type in −2.14.

This will give us the shape we are looking for here.

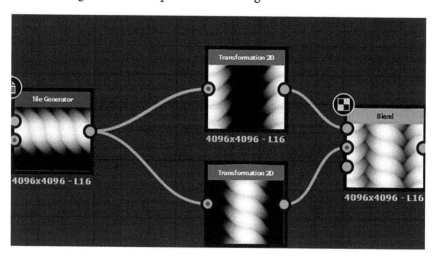

If you go into the 2D View and press the Space bar, you can see how the pattern is now tiling:

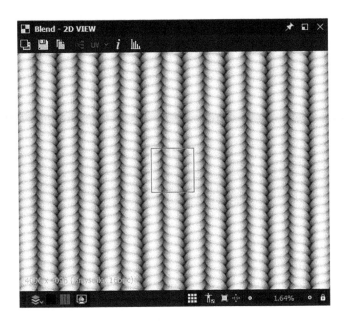

I am going to change my scale in the tiling generator to 1.24 as I want a little more gap between my weaves, but one thing that will also help is to use a rotation random value. This will give us slight randomizations in the weaves so that it is not so neat. You can also increase the position randomly in the Y and X values.

I am going to use a directional warp to add a little more randomness to the pattern. I will use a Perlin noise for the intensity input.

I will set my intensity value to 20 and turn my degrees slightly so that it is at 172, but you can change the angle any way you want, and this just adds more variation at this point.

For the Perlin noise, I changed the scale down to 8 and that seemed to do what we needed the pattern to do.

Now we are going to start adding some smaller details now, so we are going to go further back into the graph and add some fuzziness to the pattern itself.

Between the levels node and the tile generator, I am going to add a blend node. Here I will use the creased node and plug that into a Transformation 2D node. With that, I will blend that into the foreground and the levels node into the background. I will change the opacity value to 0.17, and the blending mode to subtract. This should now give us a much more subtle fabric look to what we currently have.

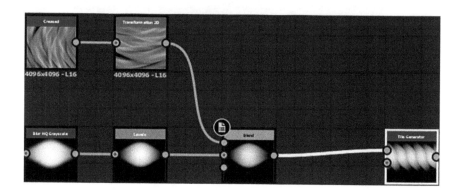

Just before we finalize this, we are also going to add a Fur 1 node with a Transformation 2D node to rotate 90cw.

Plug that into a Blend Node Foreground and plug our current shape (before the tile generator) into the background, change the opacity to something low (I am using 0.06) and the blending mode to Min (Darken) which will add some 'bump' to our thread. I have also scaled up the fur in the Transformation 2D node so play with the scale until you get something you like.

One last thing we need to do is to add some stray hairs to our shape; for this, we are going to use a tile sampler.

I am going to change the X and Y amounts to 17.

I will reduce the X size to 0.07 and Y size to 35.

I will then change my position random to around 3.3 and rotation random to 0.42.

Adjusting the scale random will allow us to have different size threads as will also Reducing our Scale to around 0.4

Let us add a directional warp and use another Perlin noise to warp our threads into something that fits our pattern a little more.

In our final directional warp, I will add a blend node and change the blending node to Max (lighten), and this will put some strands into our pattern.

Now I need to get it to tile more. Sticking it into a tile generator will give us some bad tiling artefacts, so instead, we need to use another Transformation 2D node to add some extra tiling amounts.

If you click on the /2 in the Transformation 2D node, it will scale it up ×2, giving us more resolution to use. Push your normal map intensity to around 4 and we should start seeing some good results in the 3D view.

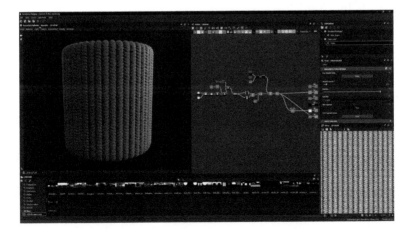

Whilst I work on this, I have added an ambient occlusion to get some more detail.

Now we can start working on the albedo settings.

To start on the albedo, I will take a curvature smooth from the normal map and add a gradient node to it.

Google is still your best friend for finding colours. I have used this awesome image of a mustard sweater for sale.

And it produced some great results for me!

Pro Tip: Adding an HSL will allow us not only to adjust the colour if we need but also to re-colour it completely using the same levels on the gradient but changing the hue completely.

Although this is looking great, there are still some things we can add or change for better results.

I want to change the roughness values because they are way too rough for this type of fabric currently. So first I will use my albedo to get my roughness values. Before I do this, I will add an ambient occlusion and blend it over my albedo slightly just to get some shading in my albedo (nothing that will break my PBR values).

I have put my ambient occlusion into a gradient and plugged it into a blend node with my fabric albedo in the background. I also changed the blending mode to multiply and reduced the opacity to 0.3. This gives me a good overlay of shadows but still sticking to PBR guidelines.

Now obviously you should know by now anything that is black in the roughness texture will be very shiny and anything that is white is smooth (dull).

I am going to use a grayscale conversion from my albedo output, and I will use an invert grayscale node to invert the colours. This will give me white cavity information where the strands meet each other (this is because this will be the LEAST shiny place in the material).

I am going to use a levels node, and in the levels node, I am going to push my black values up and white values down slightly to give me more contrast.

Then I will use the value of the mid-level to give more contrast between the strands and the fibres.

In this case, we want shiny fabric not rough fabric, so we still want dark areas but not too dark. This seems to be a good value amount here.

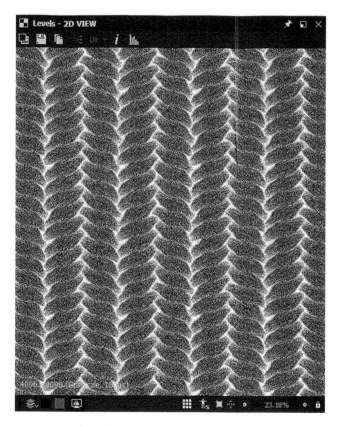

One area we need to look at before we go any further is subsurface scattering.

You may know what subsurface scattering is, but if you do not here is the gist.

Subsurface scattering (SSS) is a mechanism of light transport in which light that penetrates the surface of a translucent object is scattered by interacting with the material and exits the surface at a different point.

The light will generally penetrate the surface and be reflected a number of times at irregular angles inside the material before passing back out of the material at a different angle than it would have had if it had been reflected *directly* off the surface.

In short, anything that will scatter light needs to have an SSS Texture map. These include fabrics, skin, hair, foliage, some windows, liquid, and some terrains such as Ice and Snow.

Now the problem here is, we cannot really see SSS in its glory inside of Substance Designer.

You can enable subsurface scattering by going to Material > Default > Physically_Based_Metallic_Roughness_SSS

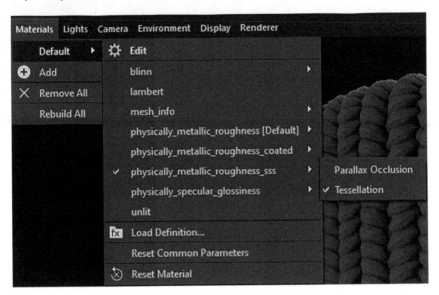

To add subsurface scattering, you need to add an output node and click on Add Item +

Then change the usage to scattering.

With that done you can plug a map into the output.

Firstly, you need to think of an SSS map as you would Roughness. Darker pixels will tell the subsurface scattering to NOT reflect light as much. Whereas Lighter pixels will allow light to travel through the surface and scatter.

You can do this either by using black and white information or colour. If you decide to use colour SSS maps, be warned that the light that travels through your surface/material will be the colour you have in the texture, whereas if you use black and white information, you can potentially change the colour (for instance, in unreal, you can create a multiply node and use a Constant 3 Vector) in engine.

Here I will use black and white because I will be finalizing the Substance Designer tutorials by giving you a few extra tips and tricks in a very good rendering software: Marmoset Toolbag.

Plug your output and save all your textures. You can do this by right-clicking on your project and clicking on Export out Bitmaps.

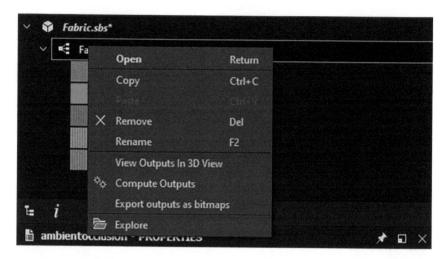

If your SSS map is not showing up in your export, simply click on the Floppy Disk Icon in the 2D View and save the texture that way.

CHAPTER 5

Rendering and Foliage

5.1 RENDERING IN MARMOSET

To finalize the portion of materials, you should know how to render your materials in a professional way.

For me, I render my materials/assets inside a Marmoset Toolbag.

First, I will open Maya and create a sphere. This should already be UVed, and I can export it straight out as a physically-based rendering (PBR) ball.

I can also create a cube and UV Unwrap all faces to fill up my Entire UDIM.

Once I have done that, I will use > Mesh > Smooth and use a value of 2 or 3. This will create a PBR ball that has near-perfect UVs for materials.

Straight Into Marmoset

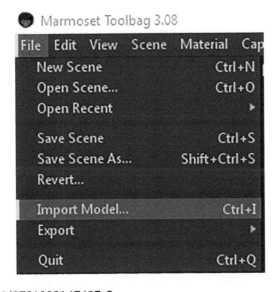

File > Import Model…

Import the PBR ball you are going to use to render this material. When you import, you will have two materials on the right side.

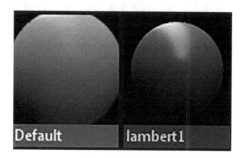

By default, your object will use lambert1, but you can change the material by simply dragging and dropping it onto your 3D model.

Let us build our material:

First, on the right, you will see a list like:

- Texture,

- Subdivision,

- Displacement,

- Surface,

- Microsurface,

- Albedo,

- Diffusion,

- Reflectivity,

- Reflection,

- Secondary Reflection,

- Occlusion, Emissive,

- Transparency and Extra.

Right now, we only need to worry about a few.

Add your albedo texture by clicking on the chequered image.

You will notice your Microsurface saying Gloss:

Click on Gloss and you can change it to Roughness.

One thing I find is that you need to flip your Y channel when you bring a normal map into Marmoset. (This could be because it uses OpenGL; however, I have noticed a lot more recently that substance seems to give you OpenGL files that should be DirectX.)

Now we need to expand subdivision and change the setting to PN triangles.

Click on the down arrow next to displacement and change it from None to Height.

Add your displacement map and change the Scale Centre to 0 and the scale to around 0.045.

After the subdivision, make sure to add an occlusion and turn the intensity down, and we do not need to worry about a cavity map for now.

Before we go further, we need to sharpen the scene more. Each texture has a settings icon next to it; let us disable all of the Mipmaps for now (we do not need LODs in our textures).

Now, before we start changing more, we will need to find a good environment to render in.

On the top left, you will see 'Scene'.

Under that, you will see 'Render'.

First, we need to click on that and change the Render settings.

Change the resolution from 1:1 to 2:1 (double).

That will give you Standard Resolution, and change the Anti-Aliasing to 0.

Under Lighting, turn on Local Reflections and Internal Refraction.

Under Global Illumination, enable GI, Diffuse, Specular, Secondary Bounces and Occlusion Detail to ×4.

Put Voxel Resolution to High and also turn on Tessellation.

Make sure you use Show Voxels to get the voxels to fit your scene.

The Voxel scene here looks fine.

Enable the ambient occlusion and turn the strength up slightly.

Now, let us look at our environment scene; you will find that under 'Sky'.

Click on sky and under Sky Light, you will see Presets.

Click on the Presets to see a list of pre-loaded, pre-made presets for Marmoset.

You can also add your own if you know how, but I will not go into that now.

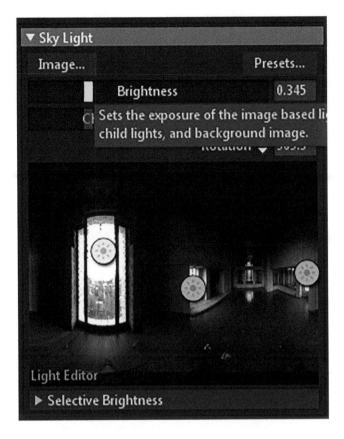

I have chosen this scene. If you left-click anywhere in the image, you will see that Marmoset adds that specific area as a light source (this can help with bounce lights); at this point, I am happy with this.

Next, I will go to Diffusion under my material settings and change it from Lambertian to Subsurface Scatter or Microfiber; for this, I used Microfiber.

I added my SSS map and turned the Fuzz and Scatter to 1, and occlusion is at 0.

I will also change Specular to Adv. Metalness and then turn down my specular amount.

Now on to Main Camera.

If I click on that, I get a whole new bunch of settings.

Firstly, I will go to Safe Frame.

This will show me if my Render is in or not.

Next, I will go to my Capture > Settings at the top.

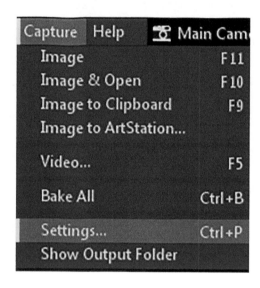

For materials, it is good to render at a 4,096 × 4,096 width or higher.

You will notice that the moment I change the width and height to 4,096, the frame changes its shape too.

You will have to type the values by default; however, there is a drop-down list on the right that has a few preset settings.

We are going to put our sampling up to 400× and our format to JPEG.

Now just click on OK, and we are good to go.

Next, we are going to change the Post Effect Settings.

Change the exposure to 0.69 or 0.8.

I turned my contrast up to 1.015.

Also, I changed my sharpen strength to 0.5.

When you are ready, click on Capture and click on Image. You can also press F11. The output folder by default is the desktop, but you can specify where you want to save.

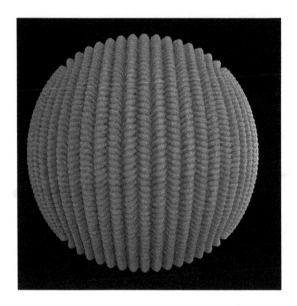

5.2 A LOOK AT FOLIAGE

Although this book is heavily based on Substance Designer, it is good to get a little knowledge of all areas, so we are going to take a look at another process that an Environment Artist will do on a daily basis: creating foliage.

Environment Art Foliage:

We are using Megascans Assets as a base for us to improve/add. Let us start from the beginning: open up Quixel Bridge (it is worth noting that if you have Unreal Engine 4 installed, you will have access to the entire library for free).

Select; > Home > 3D Assets > Tree > Trunk (see the image below):

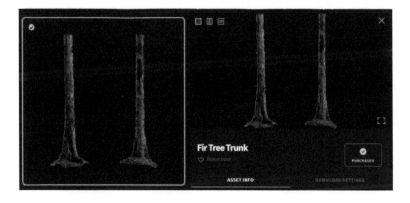

For this lesson, we are going to use Fir Tree Trunk; you can also find this on the website.

You can find out which one by left-clicking on the image in Bridge.

Once we have downloaded, we are going to navigate to our download folder; my folder is here: G:\Megascans\Downloaded\3d\tree_assembly_tk3sfemda

NOTE: You need to select your own download folder.

Alright, so let us get down to the nitty-gritty now. Let us start by opening Maya™.

We need to import our base into Maya, so let us start easy. Select > File > Import >

Select: tk3sfemda_LOD0.fbx

Now we should have our base model in Maya™.

Let us make sure the UVs are good by applying a texture to the tree. Select the tree and in the Attribute Editor scroll to the right until you find lambert1. Left click on Colour, then choose File.

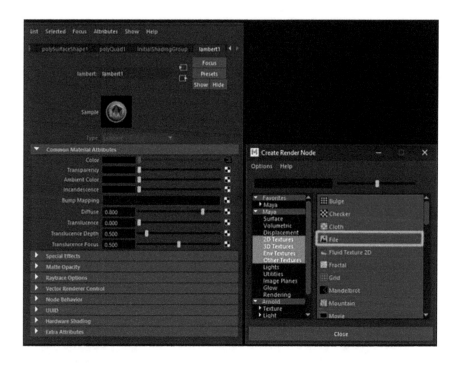

Now, all we need to do is click on the Folder icon (the image below) and choose our albedo.

If we now press 6 on the keyboard whilst in the Maya viewport, we can see the trunk with a texture on it.

Exporting the Bark:

Add a cylinder to the scene. Under Poly Modeling you can find pCylinder. Now, in the Attribute Editor find polyCylinder1.

Here we can change settings for our cylinder. We want to make sure that Subdivisions Caps is set from 1 to 0 and let us also change Subdivisions Axis from 20 to 32. Select the top and bottom face of the cylinder and delete.

Once that is done, we are going to shape our cylinder similar to our bark upper part.

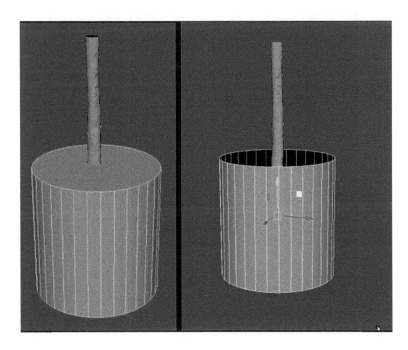

Now, we are going to make sure that our object is a live surface.

To do this, select your asset and then click on the Magnet icon (the image above). Now that our object is a live surface, we are going to add some extra edge loops to our cylinder (whilst the live surface is enabled, our cylinder surface will snap to the tree stumps surface). To add loop cuts, open your modelling toolkit and select the Multi-Cut tool, where your cursor will turn into a Knife icon.

If you hold Ctrl, you can use an entire edge loop instead of the knife cutting tool. Then instead of left-clicking, we are going to use the middle mouse button and this will add loop cuts to the centre of our surface.

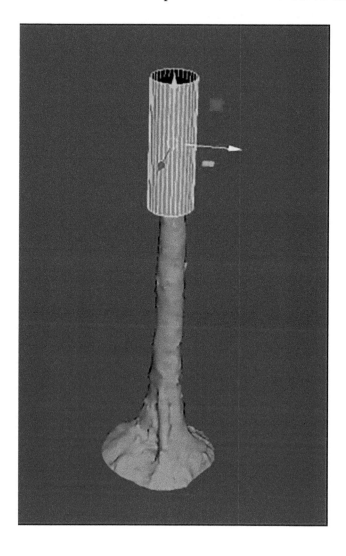

Now we need to ensure that the UVs of our Trunk (low) are lined up properly. If you want to open the UV Editor, you can find this in the Topbar > UV > UV Editor. Now select the UV Shell (hold right-click and find UV Shells). Then scale to the same size as the UV Grid 1 (UDIM 1).

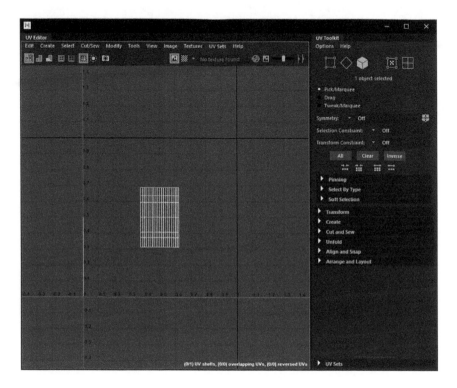

With our Trunk (low), select it and hold: Spacebar > Lighting & Shading > Transfer Maps.

Next, we need to add our Trunk to the Target Mesh and the Megascans Trunk to the Source Mesh.

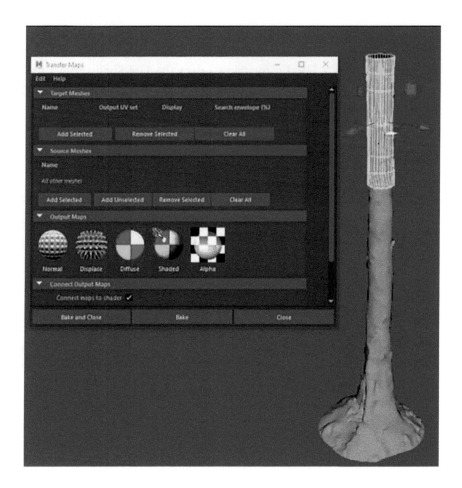

Next, we are going to select Diffuse under Output maps.

Change the format to TGA from DDS, and under Maya Common Output, we are going to change the map width and height to 4,096 (it is best to work 4K or higher and downscale afterwards).

Make sure to choose an output folder and click on Bake. Once you have baked the Diffuse/Albedo, you can view it.

Repeat this step by placing the normal map in the colour texture and bake the texture map. Then repeat with roughness and displacement (as any normal or displacement we bake from the normal will only be topology, not the texture map, we just want to flatten the texture).

There is also another alternative method to baking (which I prefer if you have the tools).

For this method, you will need Marmoset Toolbag™.

Export the Megascans Our Trunk as Separate FBX Files.

To do this in Maya: File > Export Selected (make sure only one trunk is selected). Now, in Marmoset Toolbag™: File > Import Model > Import Megascans Trunk First.

Now, let us do the same with our low-poly transfer trunk. Next, we need to set up the Baking Process. Left-click on the Loaf of Bread, and add the high trunk to the high and the low poly to the low.

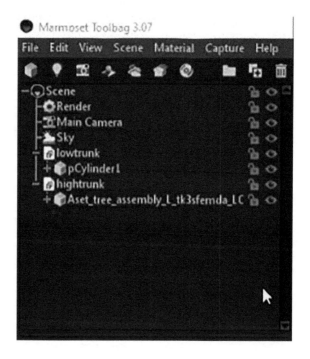

This process is the same as Maya, and we need to bake all texture maps using our albedo. So, let us start with the Diffuse. Select: configure under maps and only check the albedo.

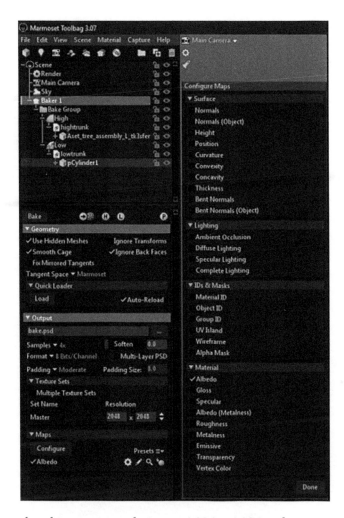

Let us also change our resolution to 4,096 × 4,096 and turn our samples down to ×1 (this will give us a sharper bake). Once we are done, just hit Bake!

Do not forget to add the Normal map into the Albedo map of the high poly and transfer only the albedo.

(Rename the baked version and bake again until you have all maps.)

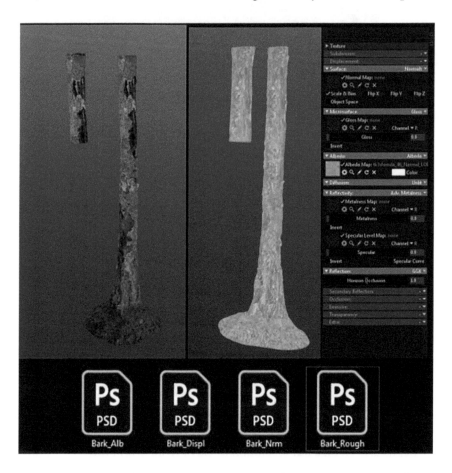

Now we need another program. Let us use Substance Painter™. First let us create a special plane in Maya. Create an image plane and then set the subdivisions to 1. This will give us a uniform UV, Duplicate repeatedly and move into position next to each other (that way, we can use the middle as our tile area).

Now we are ready for Substance Painter™.

The reason we are using Substance Painter™ is that it is great for clone painting and controlling our bark tiles.

Import our tile plane; File > New >

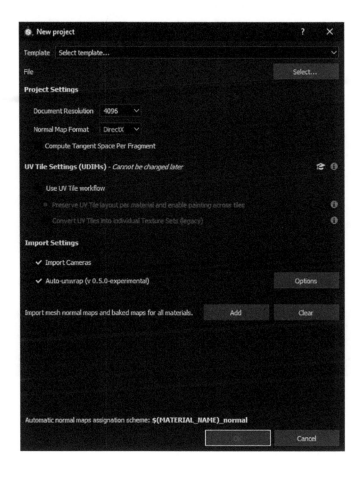

Click on Select, choose our plane and then click on OK.

At first, you may not see anything in the viewport.

That is only because our plane is flat; so hold ALT+Left Mouse Button to rotate around, and the controls are similar to Maya.

Now let us import our textures.

Import Resources > add resources > navigate to your folder and choose all texture maps.

Left-click on Undefined and change Undefined to Texture.

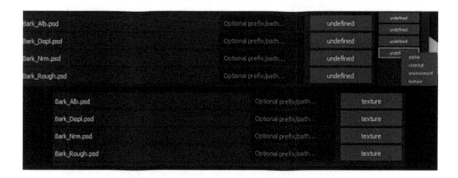

Select the dropdown and choose Project, and then select Import.

Now let us set up our base material.

On the right side of the Viewport, you can see LAYERS (this is similar to Photoshop). Delete the Layer 1 and add a fill layer.

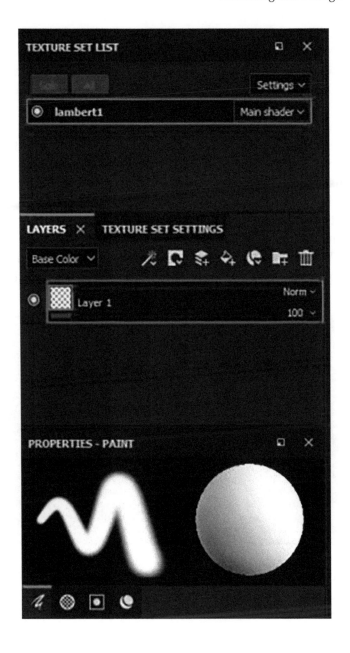

Now drag all of the textures to the matching area, i.e. Albo to Base Colour, Normal to Normal, etc.

Now we are going to create an empty layer above our fill layer.

Next, change all of our settings [Base Colour, Normal, Roughness, Height, etc.] from the norm to pass-through.

Now on the left side, you will see the Clone Stamp Tool.

All we need to do now is clean up the tiling and try to make it look less repetitive. Remember that some barks are very hard to save.

In this situation, half of the bark has been eaten by mites, so we can only save one half.

Luckily firs are very full, so it will not be fully noticeable, but that does not mean that we should not try.

Press V on an area to start copying and then just draw as you would in Photoshop. This will be a long and tedious process but well worth it.

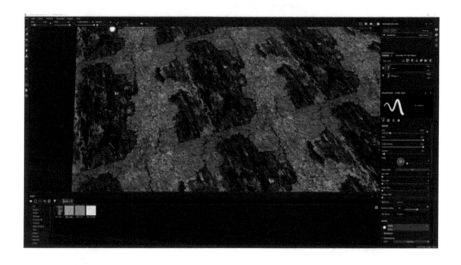

Our goal is to minimize the amount of repetition on the tileable texture.

With that done, go to File > Export Textures.

Click on this button to choose your destination folder for export.

Keep it as a PNG to start; PNG holds lossless information so that we will not lose any.

We do not need to change the config because we are exporting just the textures, so just select Export.

Now I am going to open Photoshop™ and change the resolution to 4,096 × 2,048 Image > Image Size.

Make sure to invert the textures.

The top of our texture is the bottom of the Megascans Trunk.

Image > Image Rotation > Flip Canvas Vertical Then Save the Images.

Back in Maya™, we are going to finish the trunk now.
The cylinder we used is a great shape to start with.
Create an image plane; Create > Free Image Plane

Now let us add this above image.

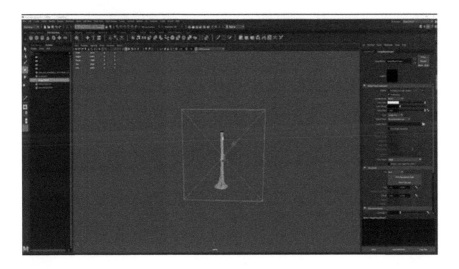

Scale the cylinder up so that it is as tall as the silhouette.

Start by adding the tileable bark texture, so we can see how it looks. Good. Now, we need to tile our bark so that it is not so stretched. In the UV Editor, select our UV Shell and scale up on the Green Axis.

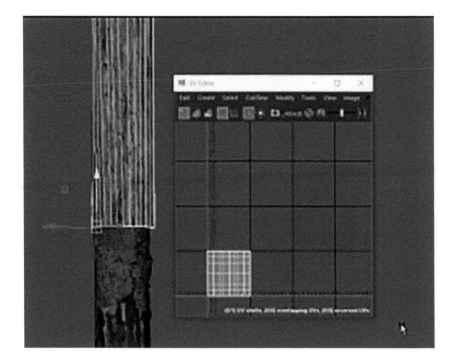

All we have to do now is attach the top trunk to the Megascans Trunk and add some more topology and shape the final trunk.

First, select both Mesh elements and hold the Spacebar > Mesh > Combine.

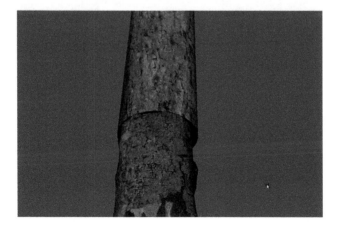

Now in the Modelling Toolkit, there is a tool called Target Weld. We are going to use this to weld the vertices of our low trunk to our high trunk.

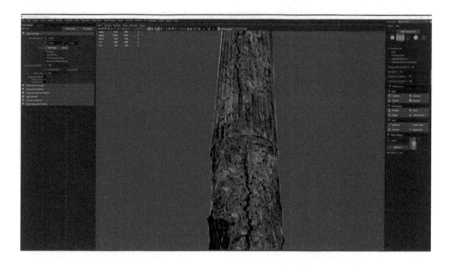

Once it is attached, let us go ahead and shape the top to match the image. Select the top vertices and scale in on all axis simultaneously.

Scale all the way down until you have the silhouette correct.

Now that we are done with the trunk, we need to build our high-poly branches; however, we cannot use these high-poly branches in a game.

So we are going to go ahead and bake them onto image planes and use lower polygonal Mesh.

We are going to carry on using Quixel with pine branches and pine family. Let us start with the branches.

Create a plane in Maya™. In the Attributes, select the material, click on the chequered box next to Colour and choose the Branch Albedo.

Now click on Transparency and choose the Opacity.

Now with our plane, we are going to use it as a starting point.

Click and Select, we want to use Click on next to.

This will open a toolbar. Make sure that we are using 3 Cubic.

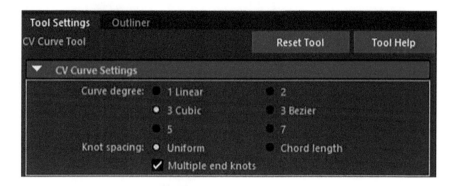

Now the rest is pretty simple.

Using this, we are going to trace the shape of our branches one by one.

Make sure that each curve has at least four points in order for it to become usable.

When you have finished your curve, press W or enter to Finalize.

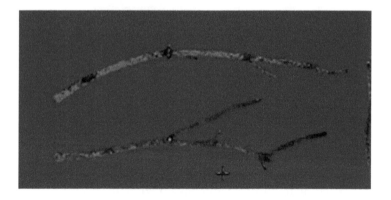

Now we do the same on any extra branches. Follow from the branch spine to create a new spine.

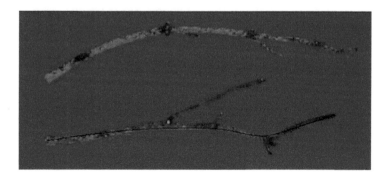

Continue until all branches are built.

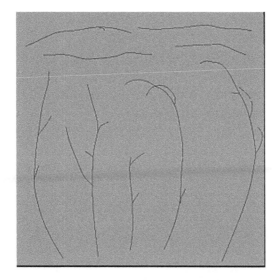

Now for another tool. We are going to use a Nurbs Circle.

Click then and choose With the Circle Selected first, Select a Spline of a Branch Then use, Be sure to select Now we are going to set up our extrude along a curve.

Follow the image below and you will not have any issues.

Make sure in the Tessellation Controls you use PER SPAN #, not PER SURF #.

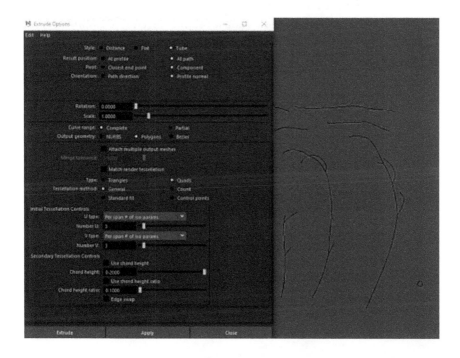

Once that is done, we can click on Apply. Repeat this step until all branches are done.

NOTE: You can make multiple different sized Nurbs Circles for different parts of the branches.

If you have any black geometry like I do, do not be alarmed all we need to do is reverse the normals or the curve.

Select the curves and go to > Curves > Reverse Direction.

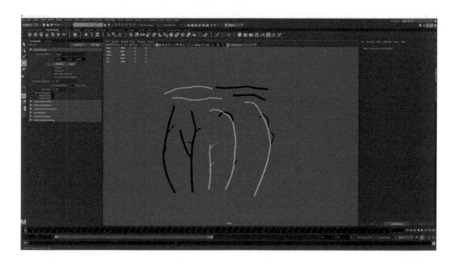

Now that we have all this done, we are going to do a few adjustments by selecting the curve. Hold the right mouse button and choose Control Vertex.

Select the vertex and move so that we have a little more shape than just flat branches.

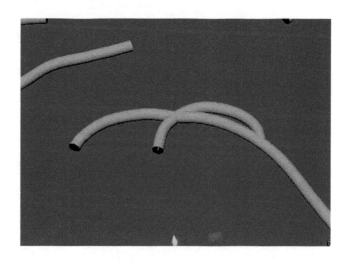

Once we have finished shaping, select each branch and combine them all together.

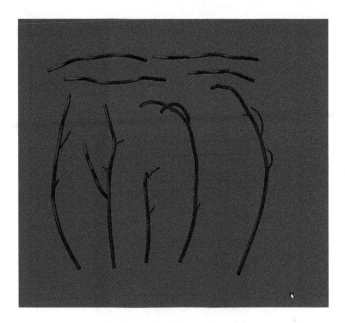

With the branches merged, we can do one last quick Edit before moving out of Maya™. Let us turn on proportional editing by pressing B.

You can either change the Falloff Radius in the settings or hold B and left mouse button + drag to change size.

Add some extra volume to the branches, and we are ready to go.

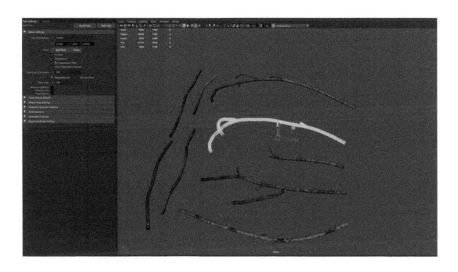

Export the objects as OBJ using > File > Export Selection.

Make sure that they are OBJ as our next program is Zbrush™. First in Zbrush, we are going to import our branches using the Import tab on the right side of the Viewer.

Left click and drag when we first bring in our mesh as nothing will be visible.

Then we are going to make sure to enable EDIT quickly so that we do not mess up our Viewport.

Now we are going to use a tool called Dynamesh.

This will retopologize our current mesh whilst keeping the shape. It will close any holes and give us a higher polycount.

You click on the right in the Subtools tab to see the Sub-Options.

We want to use DYNAMESH.

we want to change the resolution to 256 (this will give us a standard base amount to work with).

Once we have changed the resolution, click on the Dynamesh button and watch the magic.

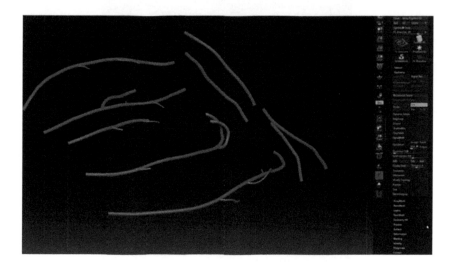

Now our holes should be closed and the branches should join one another.

We are going to sculpt our mesh now, but before we do, we need to create a brush. Open Photoshop™ and create a 2,048 × 2,048 image.

Place your height into it.

Now we are going to change the levels so that it is darker.

Now we are going to create a copy by selecting the layer and pressing CTRL+J.

Double-click on the copy and a layer style will open up. Choose gradient overlay and use the settings as below:

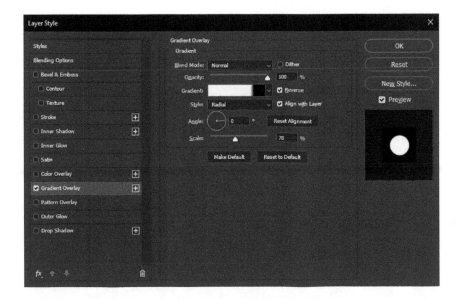

Scale is set to 96%.

Move the white part of the gradient farther over to the darker area giving us a white circle in the preview.

Right-click and rasterize the image to have a gradient like:

Make sure that the image is set to multiply:

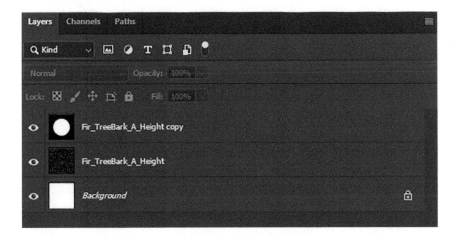

and save this image as a.BMP.

Now inside Zbrush™, import the alpha using the standard brush: click on Import.

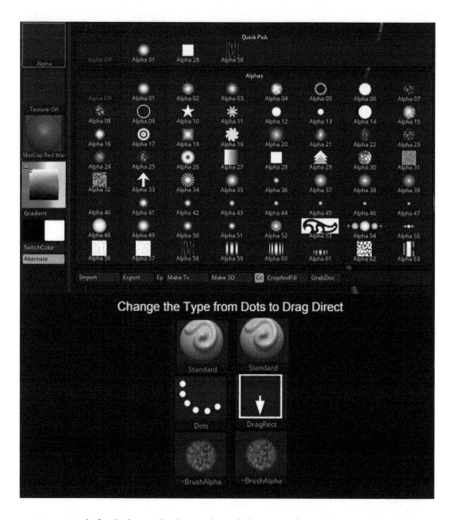

Now just left-click on the branch and drag, and I will start adding more detail (if it looks blurry, press Ctrl+D) to add more resolution.

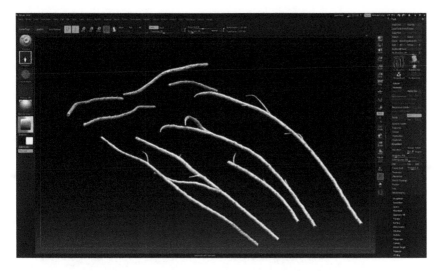

When you are finished, click Export and save out a high poly.

Back in Maya™, we need to import the High.

Apply the texture, and we now just need to shape our branches.

Create a plane and attach the Needles Texture to the plane.

Now we can trace the needles and cut them out.

Do not worry about polycount here.

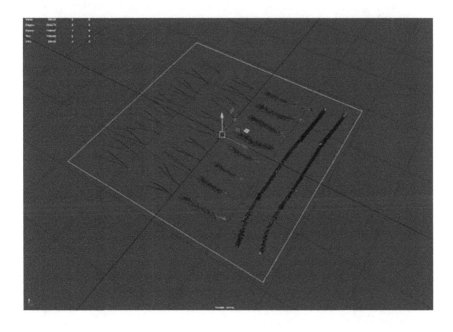

Separate each needle before cutting them out.

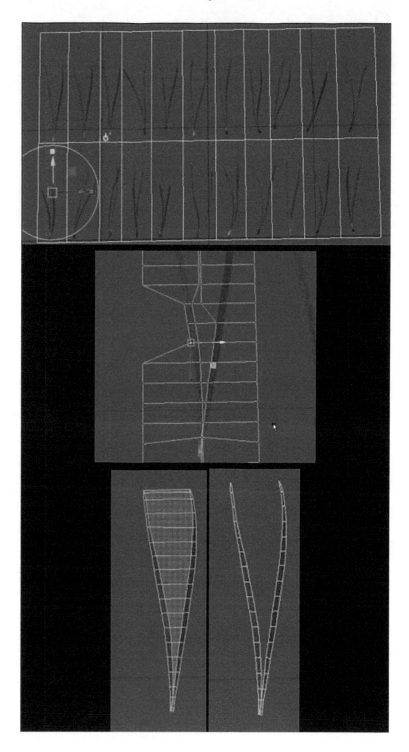

Cut off any extra geometry so that we are left with just the needles, and repeat with the rest.

Once you have done this with all of the needles on an Atlas, extrude the selected faces on the needle to create thickness like:

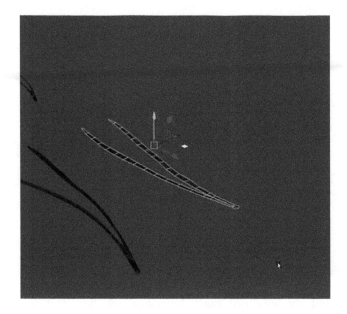

Once you have smoothed all of your pine needles out, the next step is to place them all over your branch. You can either manually place these for maximum result or procedurally place them.

Once you have finished building the branches, you will have something that looks a lot more realistic.

You will also quickly understand why we have to make our trers low poly when you see the polycounts' range between 15,000 and 2,000,000.

Now that we have our main branches, we can start to build full branches: copy the branches and start placing them together to create one large branch.

We now have one of our branches made; repeat this step as many times as you see fit. A good variation is around five to six branches.

We are going to use four branches to build larger variations too.

Now, with all of our branches, we need to create a plane that will 'wrap' around the branches. This will allow us to create the bake.

Use an orthographic view to make sure your branches fit within the plane.

Then subdivide the plane several times allowing us to shape the plane.

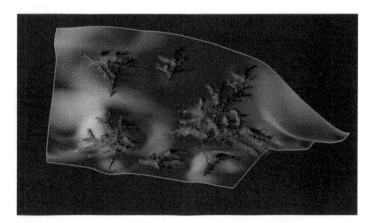

With our branches wrapped, we can now go to our baking software. Either we can do this in Maya using Transfer maps or we can do this in Marmoset.

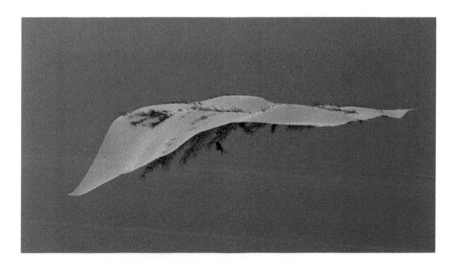

In Marmoset, we are going to select the Bake icon. This will allow us to organize our branches for the baking process.

Place the high-poly branches in the high group and the low-poly branches in the low group. Select Baker, and you will now have a list of output options. Here we can configure what we want. I am going to select Normals, Height and Albedo.

Choose your output path and bake.

Once we have all of our bakes, we can go into Photoshop and do some final touch-ups. Let us start with the albedo.

First, we need to separate the albedo from the background: drag and drop the Alpha. With the Alpha selected, we want to make a mask on our original albedo. If we copy and paste our Alpha mask, we can paste it into the mask that was selected.

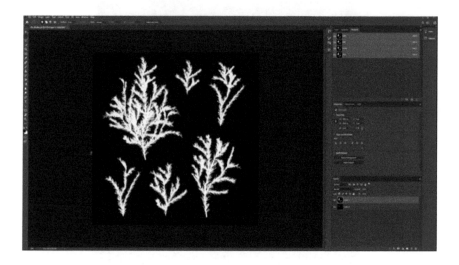

Now, Ctrl + left click on the Alpha, and this will highlight our selection. Duplicate the selection so that we no longer have a background.

Now we can create a new background through Gaussian Blur (this technique is called the Bleed method). Select your base layer and duplicate ×3 (Ctrl + J), merge the three duplicates together (Ctrl + E) (keeping the original albedo at the top), and repeat this step. You will soon notice the background bleeding in. After each duplicate, you should go to Filter > Blur > Gaussian Blur – start off at 5, then go up to 10, then 20 and then 30 on each set.

Once you have finished, you will have something that looks like this.

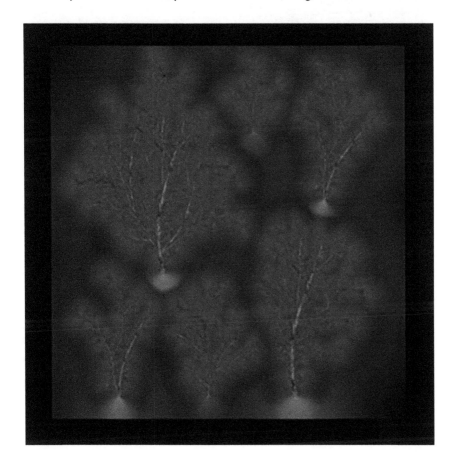

This will now allow for a good bleed on any mapping on the Alpha. Adding additional information to the foliage will be helpful; so here, we are going to add the AO and Curvature. Repeat this step with the Normal map and create the roughness from the albedo.

Now we should be good to go!

For our last step, we need to finally create the branches that will act as our low-poly branches and start dressing the tree.

Create a plane in Maya, now let us add the colour and Alpha so that we can see what we are doing!

Now let us cut out our branches and create some silhouette for them!

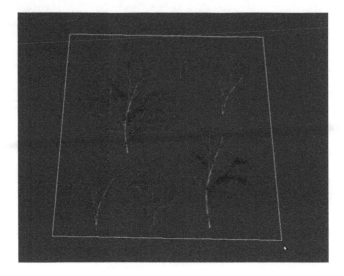

Now we are going to use soft selection to shape them into a ^ shape.

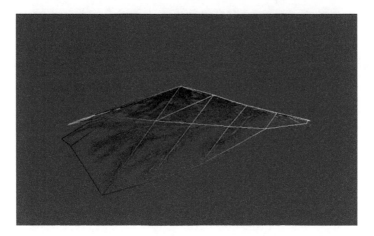

Repeat this step until you have all of your low-poly branches made.

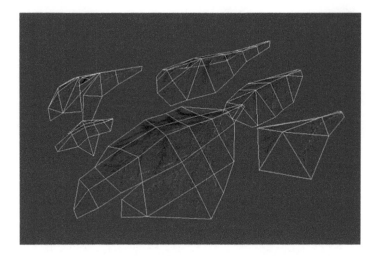

Now we just need to place a few variations together to create an extra silhouette. Now we are going to start shaping the tree by positioning the branches.

Finish shaping your tree to have a silhouette that can bring a forest to life.

Repeat this process by shortening the trunk of the tree and making a thicker fir.

Adding variation will give you multiple variations of the same tree.

5.3 DETAIL BENDING FOLIAGE

If you have ever used Cryengine, you will know that although it is an amazing engine, it is not very user-friendly and it is not set up for performance.

Over the years, I moved from Cryengine to Unreal Engine and learned that you can do anything in any engine. What I did was re-create how Cryengine would do their detail bending inside of Unreal Engine 4.

It was not the best, but it worked.

In this lesson, we are going to learn a more advanced version of Creating Plants. For this, we are going to use Maya. Eventually, we will bring this into Unreal Engine 4 and let the magic really happen! Let us start by opening Maya.

The first thing we are going to do in Maya is to create a plane in our Viewport: left-click (LMB) on the Plane icon in our Poly Modelling Tab.

Also, we're going to just want a simple plane without subdivisions. In our Attribute Editor, there will be a tab called polyPlane1. Left Click (LMB) here.

We want to drag our subdivisions Height and Width down from 10 to 1.

Now that we have that done in our Lambert tab, we can add an albedo (base colour) and an opacity (Alpha mask).

Click on the little chequered box next to Colour.

(See IMG 3.) This will bring up a Create Render Node window, where we can select the type of image. Select File.

Now we will have a file1 tab in our Attribute Editor.

Under File Attributes we can see; Image Name Left Click (LMB) on the Folder.

For this, I will use Sword_Ferns_01_4K_Albedo.jpg. If we press 6 on our keyboard, we will be able to see a textured mode instead of solid object mode.

(We can switch back at any time by pressing 4.)

Now we have our textured plane, but we do not have any transparency, so repeat the above steps and import our opacity map into our Transparency tab.

Now we should have a group of Alpha Masked fern fronds. Fun fact: a frond is a large, divided leaf.

In both common usage and botanical nomenclature, the leaves of ferns are referred to as fronds and some botanists restrict the term to this group.

Other botanists allow the term 'frond' to also apply to the large leaves of cycads and palms (Arecaceae).

'Frond' is commonly used to identify a large, compound leaf, but if the term is used botanically to refer to the leaves of ferns and algae, it may be applied to smaller and undivided leaves.

Fronds have particular terms describing their components.

Like all leaves, fronds usually have a stalk connecting them to the main stem. In botany, this leaf stalk is generally called a petiole, but in regard to fronds specifically, it is called a stipe. It supports a flattened blade (which may be called a lamina), and the continuation of the stipe into this portion is called the rachis. The blades may be simple (undivided), pinnatifid (deeply incised, but not truly compound), pinnate (compound with the leaflets arranged along a rachis to resemble a feather) or further compound (subdivided).

If compound, a frond may be compound once, twice or more. Now we are going to use our Multi-Cut (which can be found in our Modelling Toolkit) tool to cut around our fronds. Next, select each face individually and extract.

This can be done by either navigating to our top viewport > Edit Mesh > Extract or by pressing and holding down the Spacebar > Edit Mesh > Extract

Select the Next Face & Press:G. This will repeat the last step, and do this until all the Mesh Cards are separate. In our outliner, we can see that we now have individual fronds, but they will all have the history of our original plane, so we need to hold down our middle mouse button and drag each individual frond above its group. Now we can select all of our fronds and freeze the transformations, delete the history and reset the transformations.

The next step is to create some supporting geometry to give these fronds some depth and shape. Using the Multi-Cut tool again, we can hold down Left Ctrl & Click to add a whole loop to our geometry. Repeat this step until you have something like the following images:

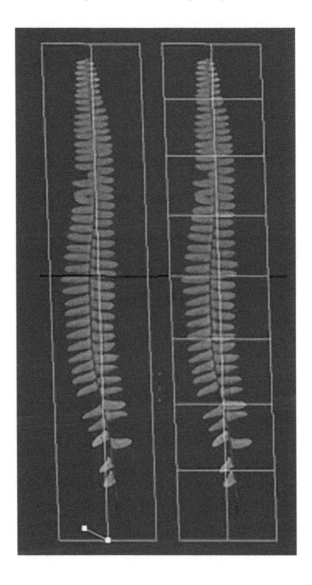

When you are happy with the shape, go into your tool settings and make sure that Preserve UVs is ticked.

Now select the vertices individually and try and eliminate most of the Alpha around the frond by moving the vertices closer to the leaves.

Also, make sure that the Middle Loop cut follows the curve of the stem:

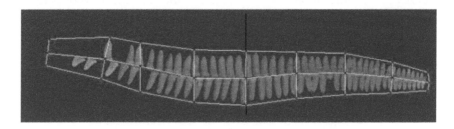

Now typically this would be more than enough in terms of geometry for our fronds or any plants in particular. However, we are going to do a more advanced version of this plant by giving it a detail bending. In order to give this plant a detail bending, we need to understand what it is we are doing.

Detail bending: Detail bending on foliage is a procedural movement caused by wind or other physical setups in the scene.

In our instance, we are going to 'fake' the wind now.

The amount that the wind influences an object is controlled by Vertex Colours.

As you can see from the image above,

- **The Red Channel:** Controls the bending at the sides of the branches/fronds.

- **The Green Channel:** Controls the delay of movement. Each individual frond/branch should be painted with a darker or lighter shade of green, and this will allow for a delayed movement.

- **The Blue Channel:** Controls the up and down movements of the branches/fronds.

With all three vertex colour channels combined, we truly do get some great results on our wind.

Here we want a proper tessellated geometry. If we have an irregularly tessellated geometry, we will get visual artefacts from the influence.

(Avoid triangles for this and use only quads.)

Add some extra supporting loop cuts to control the vertice fade amount.

Do not forget to enable Soft Selection in the Toolbar tab.

This is how Soft Selection looks like:

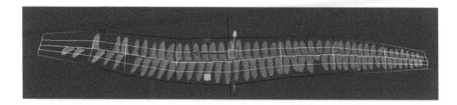

Now select the Middle Edge loop and bring the edges up with the Transpose tool. Next, select the Bottom Edge loop and make your Soft Selection radius larger. Now rotate the base until you have a frond shape.

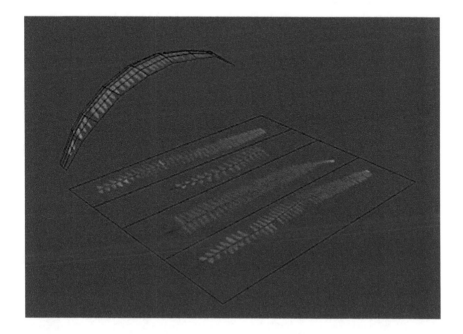

Repeat this step for the other fronds. Eventually, you will have something like the following image:

Make sure to have a variation of shapes and sizes, so that when we rotate them into the shape of a fern, they will not look weird and uniformly scaled.

Now we get into the more detailed parts, Vertex Painting! Select all of your fronds and navigate to your top toolbar: Mesh Display > Vertex Colours > Apply Colour.

(Make sure you click on the box to open the Window.)

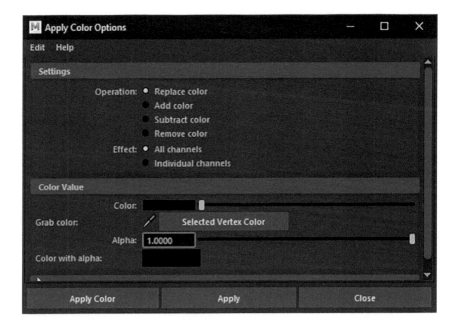

Make sure in the Settings, Operation is set to Replace Colour, Effect is set to All Channels, and the Colour is set to R: 0.000- G: 0.000- B: 0.000, which will give us Black. Select all of our fronds and left-click (LMB) on Apply.

Now that we have our Black Vertex Colours, we also need to paint our Red Vertex Colours.

Select one of your fronds and navigate your top toolbar to Mesh Display > Vertex Colours > Paint Vertex Colour Tool (make sure again to click on the box to open up the Properties). This should open the Tool Settings tab where we can see the information we want to paint; make sure that you have the operation set to add. You are painting Vertex not Vertex Face, and set the Colours to R: 1.000 G: 0.000 B: 0.000.

This will give you completely red colour.

Hover your cursor over a vertice, and you will see this little Paint Brush Circle.

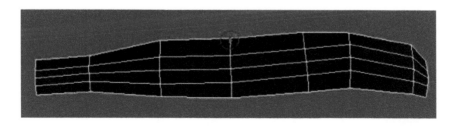

Left-click and drag up and down the edges of the vertices so that we have something like the image below:

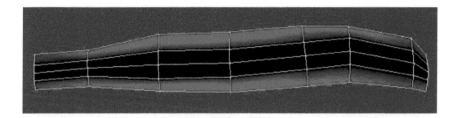

You can also fade the red edges by choosing to paint on the second set of vertices to paint down, holding down shift and doing a lighter paint.

Now repeat this step for the other fronds too.

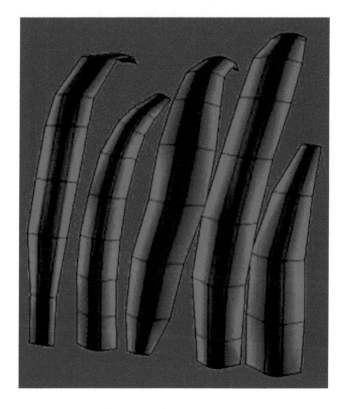

Now we are going to create our fern.

Select all of the fronds, and make sure that they are at our centre.

Navigate to our Top toolbar and select the dropdown – Modelling – and change it to Animation. Now across the Top toolbar, you will see a tab that says MASH.

Select the dropdown and click on the box to open up the Window.

We must choose Instancer as our geometry type instead of Mesh. Otherwise, we will lose the Vertice Colour information.

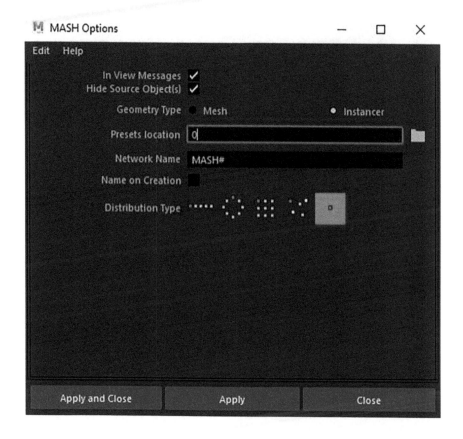

When you are happy with the settings, click on Apply & Close. Now we should see in our outliner a MASH file and a MASH1_Instancer. In our Attribute Editor, we have all of the Settings. First, we are going to select to add an ID node.

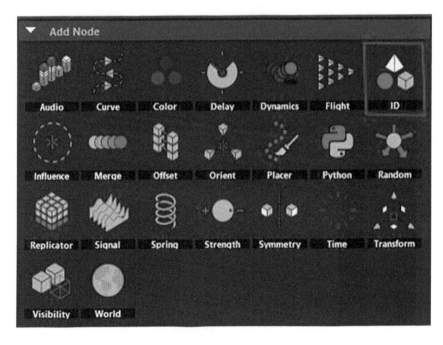

This should automatically give us an ID of 5 (as we have 5 fronds).

So depending on the number of variations you have, the ID Tab is where you will enable them to have variation.

Next, we are going to add a 'Random Node' to our MASH, which will give us the ability to control the randomizations of our plant.

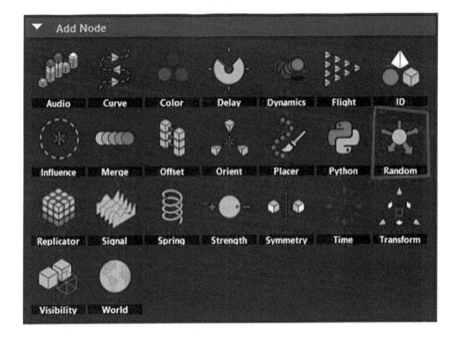

If we now navigate to our Attribute Editor, we will find the tab 'MASH1_ Distribute', which controls the number of fronds it produces and their direction and rotation.

The number of points controls how many fronds will be rendered. The distance X–Y controls the spawn point of the fronds.

The Z offset controls the spawn point of the fronds on the Z-axis. Rotating X–Y–Z controls the rotation of the fronds as they are generated.

Scaling X–Y–Z controls the scale of the fronds as they are generated offset Just slightly Offsets each individual Frond Placement.

Let us set the rotate Y (the up axis) to 360. This will give us a 360° rotation and generate our plant back in modelling mode; if we navigate our top toolbar and find: Mesh Display > Colour Set Editor and Click on it, we will get a new window with some new controls.

Hover over Display > All > and Left Click on Colour in Shaded Display.

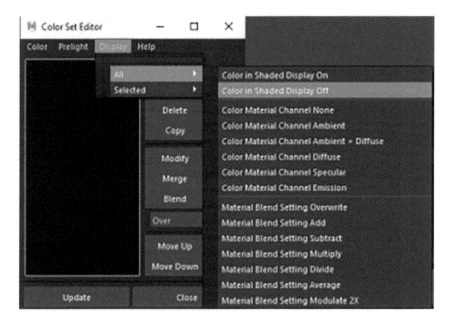

Now we can actually see what we are generating. Do not worry; we have only hidden the vertice colour information now.

Let us add some randomization to the plant now. It still seems a bit too uniform.

In the outliner, left-click on MASH & Move over to the Attribute Editor, find the MASH1_Random Node and let us play with the values.

If we randomize some of our Settings, our plant should look a little more 'natural' now.

All that is left to do is to make this a Mesh Copy and generate a few more variations. Select the MASH1_Instancer in the Outliner. Navigate to our Top Toolbar and choose Mash > Utilities > Bake Instancer to Objects. This will now make a mesh version of Our Instancer.

Now make sure that we still have our MASH1_Instancer selected and click Bake This Frame.

Now we should have a Grouped Mesh (MASH1_Instancer_objects). The good thing is they have not been joined together yet. This gives us a chance to give each individual frond a different shade of green in the Vertex Colour Information.

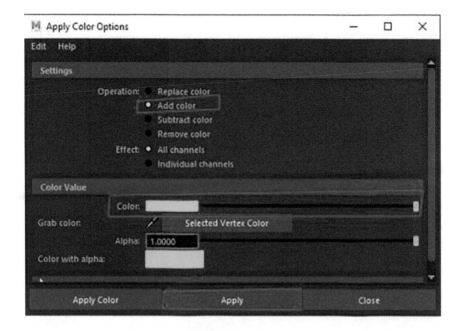

Select each frond individually and apply these settings to the frond until they are all in a shade of green. Make sure to use Add Colour and not Replace Colour as we are now combining multiple colours together.

Now we should have a plant that is with black, red and green information. Select the Entire Mesh and hold Space, and navigate to Mesh and select Combine. Navigate back to your Top Toolbar, and select Mesh Display > Paint Vertex Colour Tool (click on the Box).

Now we can paint a Radial Blue on our plant in the Tool Settings. Change the Colour Value to R: 0.000, G: 0.000, B: 1.00. Now, from a top down view, we can paint on our plant.

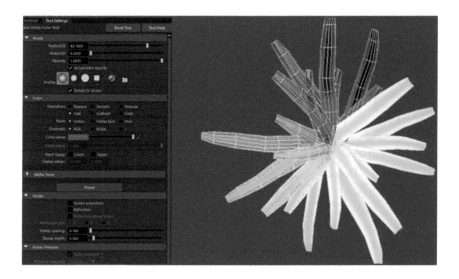

Now we can: name our plant, make a few more variations using the same technique, move our plant from the centre pivot, and reveal the MASH1_Instancer (if it's hidden).

In our Outliner, we can select MASH and choose the MASH1_ Random Tab, and then just generate random variations now with the random seed.

Repeat the above steps two or three times for a variation of foliage.

Before we Finish, after we have about three Variations of the Plant we're going to make a Few extra Variations, This time Clusters, and we'll do this by hand.

Duplicate your three ferns and Rotate, Scale and Transform them to a cluster of ferns. Now, we should have a good set of ferns.

For the rest of this tutorial series, keep an eye on my next book which will focus specifically on foliage building and different ways to optimize foliage for games and game engines whilst still keeping the visual fidelity of next-gen graphics.

Throughout this book, we have focused on very important areas within the game industry, and we explored what PBR is and how it fits into an Environment Artists pipeline in the game industry.

This is not limited to just the games industry, but it is also for cinema, etc.

We then explored Substance Designers and different types of patterns and shapes to create.

Finally, I gave you a sneak peek at some of my foliage techniques and tactics.

5.4 CONCLUSION

Throughout this book, we have explored unique and rudimentary examples of how workflows in the game industry are to be approached. We have covered the majority of this book on firstly understanding the fundamentals behind PBR. We also gave a deeper look into PBR and how the science behind it helps the game and cinema industry excel with visuals and computer graphics today.

We then looked into a very important program that is fundamental to getting a job in the industry. Since 2017, one thing an industry professional has been expected to have is Substance Designer knowledge.

We explored some basic steps. I personally learn by doing so; for example, if I watched a basic tutorial on Houdini, It would not give me the relevant information to explore, adapt and create. It would only give me a basic understanding, so I have adapted how I would prefer to learn so you can potentially take all of these techniques away and alter them to create new and improved techniques and artwork.

We looked at how to create basic shapes first by creating brick and mortar. We then dove deeper into Foliage Atlases, another important Texture/Material set to understand.

After that, we took a very simple look at trim sheets and then started diving deeper into materials, starting with rock materials. After adding some unique shapes and utilizing the ambient occlusion as a grunge mask for moss to grow, we took a look at creating a 3D material.

What is a 3D material? Hopefully, by now you will understand that a 3D material has multiple layers of materials on one Material Set; for example, here, we used the insulation, joists, and planks.

Then we dove into lava, a different kind of material that can sometimes be hard to produce, but we have given it a go!

Then finally, we looked at fabric, so now we should have an understanding of how to start off with simple shapes, create larger shapes and use those shapes to tile into bigger shapes. We can also go back over anything at any time and change parameters without breaking our entire process.

To end this book, I decided to throw in a sneak peek/helpful tutorial on foliage. Of course, I am a Principal Foliage Artist, so my area of expertise is foliage. We looked at taking a Megascans Tree Trunk and actually building it up into a final version! Using multiple programs and multiple methods, we get brilliant results. I also added in the detail bending foliage tutorial, which is amazing for adding more life to a scene, specifically inside an Unreal engine. You will notice this replication is how Cryengine use their method.

Index